PRAISE FOR M
McDONALD OI
PROPOSITIONS

'I have known Professor Malcolm McDonald for over 25 years and he has made an outstanding contribution to the marketing profession. In both strategic account management and strategic marketing he has pushed forward the frontiers of best practice. Professor McDonald's research-based frameworks are timeless and universal and have been incredibly useful to both academics and practitioners around the world. This latest book on financially quantified value propositions continues to break new ground.' **Philip Kotler, author, consultant and the S C Johnson & Son Professor of International Marketing, Kellogg School of Management, Northwestern University**

'This book is both accessible and rigorous. It is a great read for everyone involved in buying or selling. Exploring how to quantify value propositions is a stimulating and highly beneficial endeavour. McDonald and his co-authors offer real gems to the reader. This is a timely contribution to understanding how to create differentiation and develop solid collaboration in fast-changing value chains.' **Hervé Legenvre PhD, Director, Value Creation Observatory, The European Institute of Purchasing Management**

'Crafting a value proposition that firstly gets cut through and gains the attention of the intended target, and secondly motivates that person to want to know more is really the Holy Grail of all marketing because if we fail in that mission then every other marketing strategy, technique or method that we employ will do nothing more than waste time and money.

I firmly believe that there is nothing more important in the broad spectrum of disciplines that we refer to as marketing than the creation of an effective value proposition. And this is the first book that I've read that offers a proven and time-tested formula for creating a value proposition. It's written in terms that both the experienced marketer and the layperson can understand and, more importantly, can implement and thereby gain substantial benefit.' **Tom Poland, Chief Leadsologist, Leadsology**

'Value propositions are simultaneously one of the most powerful ideas in business and one of the least understood and worst executed. In this book two leading authors show how to develop, use and profit from them.' **Dr Diana Woodburn, Chairman, The Association for Key Account Management**

'It is so refreshing to see a book focused on the impact good marketing can make on profit, since so much of today's marketing discussion is about digital tools, leads and nurture flows. Anchored in tried and tested techniques, such as needs-based segmentation, McDonald and Oliver's book is action oriented. Its tools and templates will help marketers create real value for their company and its customers.' **Bev Burgess, Senior Vice President and ABM Practice Leader, ITSMA**

'Finally, here is a book that explains clearly what the concept is and how to create a financially quantifiable value proposition! You can now communicate to your ideal customers why they should buy from you (unique differentiation), how you'll improve their situation (relevancy) and how they'll financially benefit, all in language that they understand. This book will shape your strategic marketing planning.' **Stewart Barnes, Managing Director, QuoLux Ltd**

'Value is one of the most talked about and least understood ideas in business today. This excellent book provides a comprehensive review of the main concepts and also provides a series of case studies to bring the ideas alive. Malcolm McDonald and Grant Oliver pool their extensive business knowledge and experience to bring clarity, helping to define what value means to us, our business and most importantly our customers.' **Richard Ilsley, Managing Partner, Key Account Management Group**

Malcolm McDonald on Value Propositions

How to develop them, how to quantify them

Malcolm McDonald and Grant Oliver

KoganPage

Publisher's note

Every possible effort has been made to ensure that the information contained in this book is accurate at the time of going to press, and the publisher and authors cannot accept responsibility for any errors or omissions, however caused. No responsibility for loss or damage occasioned to any person acting, or refraining from action, as a result of the material in this publication can be accepted by the editor, the publisher or any of the authors.

First published in Great Britain and the United States in 2019 by Kogan Page Limited

2nd Floor, 45 Gee Street	c/o Martin P Hill Consulting	4737/23 Ansari Road
London EC1V 3RS	122 W 27th St, 10th Floor	Daryaganj
United Kingdom	New York, NY 10001	New Delhi 110002
www.koganpage.com	USA	India

© Malcolm McDonald and Grant Oliver, 2019

This book contains brand new insights at the cutting edge of marketing, in addition to celebrating previously published content from Malcolm McDonald's vast collection of authored work.

ISBN   978 0 7494 8176 6
E-ISBN   978 0 7494 8175 9

British Library Cataloguing-in-Publication Data

A CIP record for this book is available from the British Library.

Library of Congress Cataloging-in-Publication Data

Names: McDonald, Malcolm, author. | Oliver, Grant, author.
Title: Malcolm McDonald on value propositions : how to develop them, how to
   quantify them / Malcolm McDonald and Grant Oliver.
Description: London ; New York : Kogan Page, [2019] | Includes
   bibliographical references.
Identifiers: LCCN 2018030978 (print) | LCCN 2018031959 (ebook) | ISBN
   9780749481759 (ebook) | ISBN 9780749481766 (pbk.)
Subjects: LCSH: Corporate image. | Branding (Marketing) | Value. | Customer
   relations.
Classification: LCC HD59.2 (ebook) | LCC HD59.2 .M4185 2019 (print) | DDC
   659.2–dc23

Typeset by Integra Software Services, Pondicherry
Print production managed by Jellyfish
Printed and bound by 4edge Limited, UK

CONTENTS

14 **Financial analysis, value quantification tools and financial dashboards** 213

15 **Summary of the value proposition process** 231

ABOUT THE AUTHORS

Emeritus Professor Malcolm H B McDonald MA(Oxon) MSc PhD DLitt DSc

 Until 2003, Malcolm was Professor of Marketing and Deputy Director of Cranfield University School of Management, with special responsibility for e-business. He is a graduate in English Language and Literature from Oxford University, in Business Studies from Bradford University Management Centre and has a PhD from Cranfield University. He also has a doctorate from Bradford University and from the Plekhanov University of Economics in Moscow. He has extensive industrial experience, including a number of years as Marketing and Sales Director of Canada Dry. Until the end of 2012, he spent seven years as Chairman of Brand Finance plc.

He spends much of his time working with the operating boards of the world's biggest multinational companies, such as IBM, Xerox, BP and the like, in most countries in the world, including Japan, the USA, Europe, South America, ASEAN and Australasia.

He has written 46 books, including the best seller *Marketing Plans: How to prepare them, how to use them,* which has sold over half a million copies worldwide. Hundreds of his papers have been published.

Apart from market segmentation, his current interests centre around the measurement of the financial impact of marketing expenditure and global best practice key account management. He is an Emeritus Professor at Cranfield and a Visiting Professor at Henley, Warwick, Aston and Bradford Business Schools.

In 2006 he was listed in the UK's Top Ten Business Consultants by *The Times*. Email m.mcdonald@cranfield.ac.uk

Grant Oliver

Grant has been involved in the software and IT services industries for over 20 years in Europe, the USA, India, the Middle East and Australia. He has worked as a CEO, managing director, sales and marketing director, and non-executive director. His background spans a range of companies from start-ups to listed software companies.

Grant has advised software and consulting companies in the financial services, utilities and healthcare sectors on acquisitions.

Grant's experience includes:

- turnaround experience in both private and public companies;

- investment, M&A and corporate finance experience;

- advising on fundraising for a software company through venture capital and private individuals;

- non-executive director of a housing association and a solar energy company.

Grant currently acts as a mentor in the Digital Health, London Accelerator scheme coaching digital health companies.

ABOUT THE CONTRIBUTORS

Alan Crean

Alan Crean is a subject matter expert in the quote-to-cash lifecycle for services and consultancy firms. He is currently the Business Unit Executive for Changepoint PSC and PPM in EMEA.

Mark Davies

Mark is the Managing Director of Segment Pulse Limited – a consulting practice that helps organizations to create, sell and deliver innovative value propositions. He is the author of *Infinite Value*, published by Bloomsbury in 2017, and co-author of *Implementing Key Account Management*, published by Kogan Page in 2018.

Mark has co-directed the Cranfield KAM Best Practice Club since 2008 (he was previously a delegate member when he was working for BP). Through this community he has had the privilege of working with some of the leading researchers, thinkers and practitioners in the world of KAM and strategic selling for some 15 years. He is a chartered engineer, a chartered marketer, and a fellow of the Chartered Institute of Marketing.

Des Evans

Des Evans received an OBE in the Queen's 2016 Birthday Honours List for services to the motor industry. Evans stood down in July 2014 as Chief Executive of MAN Truck & Bus UK after nearly 40 years in commercial vehicle sales and marketing in the UK.

Evans joined MAN as a sales director in 1993 and, over the following 21 years, developed MAN and its UK dealer network as a leading supplier of trucks and buses, with a consistent 11 per cent share of the UK truck market. He was appointed chief executive in 2004, and throughout his time at MAN he was involved in the development of innovative finance and repair packages. A great proponent of telematics, Evans has long emphasized the importance of the driver in getting the best from today's modern trucks.

In July 2014 he was awarded the Motor Transport, Service to Industry Award. The judging panel said Evans was 'probably the single most knowledgeable and accessible CEO or MD in the UK truck industry'. They also pointed to his support for the launch of the Everywoman Transport and Logistics Awards, his backing for the IRTE's Technician accreditation scheme for workshop technicians, and his long-term commitment to overseas development charity, Transaid.

In addition to his responsibilities for the truck business, Evans oversaw the delivery of more than 7,000 MAN trucks for the British armed forces – the biggest single truck order placed in Europe in the past 25 years. He was appointed Honorary Professor at Aston Business School in October 2014 and is involved in the development of the Aston Centre for Servitisation Research and Practice.

Todd Snelgrove

Todd Snelgrove is the former Global Vice President of Value at SKF. He played the value evangelist for 20 years inside SKF, a global industrial engineering company. He worked tirelessly to help his company understand and create, price, and sell products and services that truly create customer value. He developed a systematic, best-in-class tool and methodology to quantify customer value with the SKF Documented Solutions Program, which has over 100,000 cases of approved customer value worth over US$7 billion. Snelgrove is a noted expert in selling, pricing, and buying value and now has his own consulting practice, Experts In Value, focused on helping companies that create value get paid for that value. He presents his value message at numerous global conferences, and has presented at schools such as London Business School, Cranfield, Kellogg, Macquarie, ESADE and numerous others. He co-wrote and edited the book *Value First Then Price: Quantifying value in business to business markets from the perspective of both the buyer and seller.*

An important introduction

Getting the best out of your value proposition

About this book

In some respects, this is an unusual book because it deals in a lot of detail with two domains, as shown in Figure 0.1. This figure will be shown on a number of occasions in this book, as an important contextual representation of value propositions. The main thrust of this book is preparing value propositions for major customers, shown in the top right part of Figure 0.1.

Figure 0.1 The customer portfolio

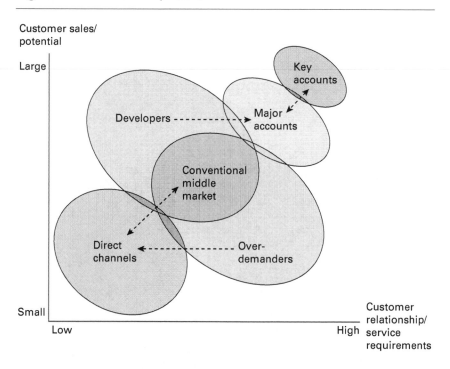

Many marketers often find themselves in the firing line with their sales colleagues by failing to prepare effective value propositions for the main markets, shown in the middle of the figure.

In an ideal world, marketers would be responsible for the whole of the 'map' shown in Figure 0.1, for example when Malcolm was marketing and sales director at Canada Dry. But, recognizing the reality of business life today, we have shown how to prepare value propositions for all parts of the map. Those who need to develop value propositions for major customers should therefore concentrate on those sections of the book. Then those who are in a marketing role and need to know how to develop value propositions for markets, sectors or segments, will likely find the others more helpful.

In this way, we have aimed to create a book where you can pick and choose the relevant sections as you move through various challenges in your professional lives, although of course we recommend reading and acting on the book as a whole for the best results.

It is also interesting to consider where this book fits into the marketing domain in general. In Chapter 4 we spell out where the value proposition process fits into the strategic marketing planning process. Over and above this, however, is the need to know where this book fits in with marketing as a discipline and as a process. Figure 0.2 is a 'map' of the total marketing process. This shows where the development of value propositions slots in and it should be noted that these are – or should be – the culmination

Figure 0.2 Map of the marketing domain

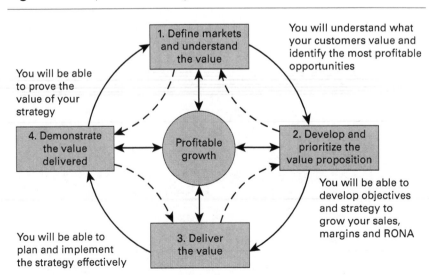

of considerable analysis completed earlier in the marketing process. Alas, in most cases, the development of value propositions is lacking, but that is where we are here to help. This book aims to fill this knowledge and action gap.

Best wishes from the authors,
Malcolm McDonald and Grant Oliver

How financially quantified value propositions will make you richer 01

Introduction

We will define more specifically what value means in Chapter 3.

First up, are you seen as being the same as most of your competitors? You certainly will not be if you read and implement the contents of this book. As the authors, we work mainly at director level in companies and can always tell when the company is either in serious financial trouble or is about to get into serious financial trouble very soon.

It really is very simple and straightforward.

We ask them two simple questions:

1 What are your key target markets, in order of priority?

2 In each, what are your organization's sources of differential advantage?

The first question is nearly always answered by the directors, immediately focusing on their *products*.

Remember IBM in the 1980s, who nearly went bankrupt because they defined their market as 'mainframes'?[1] I have discussed this broadly across the series, particularly in *Malcolm McDonald on Marketing Planning*. Gestetner, Kodak and Nokia all did similar, narrowing their markets to 'duplicators', 'films and cameras' and 'phones'. Even today there are publishers who define their market as 'books', when the reality is that business book publishers are in the business knowledge market. The pension example is another great representation: there is no such thing as the 'pensions' market. The reality is that there is the 'retirement income' market and pensions are only one way of satisfying the needs of this market, in a similar way that books are only one way of satisfying the need for knowledge about business. Particularly with the influence of digital and new channels to consumers, there are multiple ways of facilitating this thirst for knowledge, both in addition to and complementing books.

Building on this, consider for example research institutes, journalists, consultants, software houses, conference reports, online book stores, online databases, colleges and many others. Appreciating this and drawing a quantified market map of how this market works from end to end, identifying where books or phones or cameras fit in, is the first step to developing a robust marketing strategy. We will discuss this further in Chapter 6.

The graveyard of corporate deaths over the past 20 years indicates that this is not some weird, academic, theoretical notion. Today, *all* products and services are excellent – in the sense that they all work perfectly well, so having a good product will no longer deliver you the riches that you desire. No, today the only way to get rich is to differentiate yourself in a way that appeals to your customers. In many industries, one big part of this appeal to customers is *money*. If a customer knows that dealing with you will make them richer, they will deal with you. It really is that simple. The problem is, they need to know *how* they will be richer and it is your job to demonstrate this to them.

The dreaded website copy

We spend an incredible amount of our lives looking at websites, getting swamped with the same generic phrasing: innovation, better quality, a trusted reputation, responsive good results for customers, the leading provider of… and so the list goes on.

With increasing competition and active consumers with larger control over their research and decision-making, where is your differentiation in the customer's language? What problem are you solving that someone else isn't? What is parting with their time or money going to solve for them? The quality of services that you are advertising here should be inherent in this solution.

Malcolm Frank, SVP of Strategy and Marketing at Cognizant, presented the following list of examples at ITSMA's Marketing Leadership Forum. How many differentiating factors can you draw out from what these IT and IS suppliers are offering?[2]

- Global management consulting, technology services, and outsourcing company. Committed to delivering innovation, which collaborates with its clients to help them become high-performance businesses and governments.

- Comprehensive IT services integrated with business insight to reduce costs, improve productivity and assert competitive advantage.

- Provides consulting and IT services to clients globally – as partners to conceptualize and realize technology-driven business transformation initiatives.

- Provides a broad portfolio of business and technology solutions to help its clients worldwide improve their business performance. Our core portfolio comprises information technology, applications, and business process services, as well as information technology transformational services.

- No.1 provider of integrated business, technology, and process solutions on a global delivery platform.

- The world-leading information technology consulting, services and business process outsourcing organization that envisioned and pioneered the attention of the flexible global business practices that today enable companies to operate more efficiently and produce more value.

You will understand by now that the second part of the question asked of a board of directors cannot possibly be answered. Remember, this was: 'what is your organization's sources of differential advantage of each of your key target markets?'

It is to the answer of this question that this book is devoted.

By way of summary so far, let us state emphatically that any operating board that cannot answer these two simple questions should be redeployed, because any company can only survive by targeting its key target markets, understanding what they need and by meeting these needs better than another organization offering something similar.

To reiterate, these two questions are:

1 In order of priority, what are your key target markets?
2 In each key target market, what are your organizational sources of differential advantage?

The problems facing most organizations today

For any organization today, the differentiation sought by the customer is more challenging than at any time in history, but it remains at the very heart of successful marketing. If you are in an overcrowded market, where you are not distinctive, all that lowering prices achieves is to lower your margins. Just look at the following very simple example:

Price £10
Margin £2
Sell 100

Giving a 5 per cent discount just to keep the business results in the following:

Price £9.50
Profit £1.50
Sell 133.3

In other words, you need to sell a third more just to make the same amount of profit.

Giving a 10 per cent discount just to keep the business results in the following:

Price £9
Profit £1
Sell 200

In other words, you have to sell *twice* as much just to make the same margin of profit. So, why on earth would any sane person trade on price? However, our research has shown clearly that the only reason customers buy on price is because they see all suppliers as more or less the same.

Let's get the dreaded price issue out of the way

To start, here is another simple example of the effect of price. From Table 1.1, it can be seen that, all things being equal, price has the biggest impact on the bottom line, followed in second place by costs and in third place by sales. All this shows is that price always has – and always will have – the biggest impact on profits.

Being helpful and pragmatic, we have also provided Table 1.2, a crib to help you calculate the impact of price discounts at given margins.

There is, however, another major point to be made, this time about typical company accounting systems.

One of us is former marketing director of a fast moving consumer goods company. It sold 3 million items to two major retailers at approximately the same price:

Table 1.1 The impact of price on profit

	Start point	Vol + 1%	Costs – 1%	Price + 1%
Volume	1,000	1,010	1,000	1,010
Fixed costs	400	400	396	400
Variable costs	500	505	495	500
Profit	100	105	109	110
Turnover	1,000	1,010	1,000	1,010
Profit increase	0%	5%	9%	10%

- Customer A insisted on daily, just-in-time, store-by-store delivery, at great cost to the supplier. They also insisted on the sales force carrying out in-store merchandising. Worst of all, however, Customer A took about 145 days to settle their accounts.

- Customer B, on the other hand, asked for one central delivery (hence one invoice). They did not require the sales force to do in-store merchandising. Finally, they settled their accounts in 45 days.

The company's accounting system, however, like most company's accounting systems – even in 2018 – only measured product profitability, with overhead costs being allocated on the basis of volume. Consequently, both Customers A and B appeared to be equally profitable. The reality was that the supplier was rewarding Customer A for being a bad customer and penalizing Customer B for being a good customer.

The point of this true story is that it is not product profitability alone that should be calculated, but also the cost of dealing with the customer after the product has left the 'factory', that is, customer profitability. Clearly, in a book on value propositions, considerations such as this should be borne clearly in mind.

Let us make one final point about the dangers of cost-cutting in a short case overview. A number of supermarkets in the UK began cutting costs shortly after the 2008 recession had started to bite. It was a common sight for stores to begin looking worse for wear; staff were demotivated, revenue was down and accounting scandals began to emerge, in some cases with prosecution. Yet perhaps overshadowing all of this in the public eye was when horse meat was found in a number of beef products in 2013.[3] A cohort of well-known supermarket and restaurant players were caught up in the scandal, compromising their mark of quality as they drove the prices of their supplier down. The sector was rocked in outrage, nationwide testing, and

Table 1.2   How to calculate the impact of price discounts via given margins

If you cut your price	and your present gross profit is							
	5%	10%	15%	20%	25%	30%	35%	40%
	You need to sell this much more to break even							
	%	%	%	%	%	%	%	%
1%	25.0	11.1	7.1	5.3	4.2	3.4	2.9	2.6
2%	66.6	25.0	15.4	11.1	8.7	7.1	6.1	5.3
3%	150.0	42.0	25.0	17.6	13.6	11.1	9.4	8.1
4%	400.0	66.6	36.4	25.0	19.0	15.4	12.6	11.1
5%	-	100.0	50.0	33.3	25.0	20.0	16.7	14.3
6%	-	150.0	66.7	42.9	31.6	25.0	20.7	17.6
7%	-	233.3	87.5	53.8	38.9	30.4	25.0	21.2
8%	-	400.0	114.3	66.7	47.1	36.4	29.6	25.0
9%	-	1000.0	150.0	81.8	56.3	42.9	34.6	29.0
10%	-	-	200.0	100.0	66.7	50.0	40.0	33.3
11%	-	-	275.0	122.2	78.6	57.9	45.8	37.9
12%	-	-	400.0	150.0	92.3	66.7	52.2	42.9
13%	-	-	650.0	185.7	108.3	76.5	59.1	48.1
14%	-	-	1400.0	233.3	127.3	87.5	66.7	53.8
15%	-	-	-	300.0	150.0	100.0	75.0	60.0
16%	-	-	-	400.0	177.8	114.3	84.2	66.7
17%	-	-	-	566.7	212.5	130.8	94.4	73.9
18%	-	-	-	900.0	257.1	150.0	105.9	81.8
19%	-	-	-	1900.0	316.7	172.7	118.8	90.5
20%	-	-	-	-	400.0	200.0	133.3	100.0
21%	-	-	-	-	525.0	233.0	150.0	110.0
22%	-	-	-	-	733.0	275.0	169.2	122.2
23%	-	-	-	-	1115.0	328.6	191.7	135.3
24%	-	-	-	-	2400.0	400.0	218.2	150.0
25%	-	-	-	-	-	500.0	250.0	166.7

Example Your present gross margin is 25% and you cut your selling price 10%. Locate 10% in the left-hand column. Below, follow across to the column located 25%. You find you will need to sell 66.7% MORE units.

precautionary product withdrawal. The lesson here is to be highly aware of excessive cost-cutting, whatever the size of your business; the impact can be unexpected and trust is extremely difficult to win back once lost.

For now, let's agree that there has to be a better way of doing business and a key way forward is to develop financially quantified value propositions (detailed closely in Chapter 3).

Sales velocity

There are four factors that impact how much you sell. It is a function of:

1 number of leads;

2 closure rates;

3 average deal size;

4 sales cycle.

Marketing has most influence on item 1 and the sales team has most influence on items 2 to 4.

Figure 1.1 Sales velocity equation

$$\text{Sales velocity} = \frac{\text{(1) Number of leads} \times \text{(2) Closure rate (\%)} \times \text{(3) Average deal size (£)}}{\text{(4) Sales cycle (months)}}$$

SOURCE Based on the Sales Velocity Equation, reproduced with the kind permission of Donal Daly, Executive Chairman at Altify (formerly The TAS Group)

Figure 1.2 Sales velocity example

$$\text{Sales velocity} = \frac{(125 \times 20\% \times £120,000)}{3 \text{ months}}$$

$$= £1,000,000 \text{ per month}$$

By increasing closure rate, average deals size and reducing sales cycle by 10%

$$\text{Sales velocity} = \frac{(125 \times 22\% \times £132,000)}{2.7 \text{ months}}$$

$$= £1,344,000 \text{ per month}$$

An increase of 34%

Figure 1.3 Justification for value propositions

Measure	Figure
Annual sales revenue	£15,000,000
New sales	£12,000,000
Number of annual deals	100
Average discount %	10%
Number of leads annually	500
Closure rate	20%
Average deal size	£120,000
Sales cycle (days)	90
Profit margin	10%

1	Number of leads annually	
	This is mainly the responsibility of marketing. Can it be increased and by what percentage?	0%
2	Closure rate	
	A typical value proposition increases closure rate by 2–10%, estimate increase	10%
3	Average deal size	
	A typical value proposition reduces discounting by 20–30%, estimate price increase	10%
4	Sales cycle	
	A typical value proposition reduces the sales cycle by 10–25%, estimate reduction	10%

Additionally, 90 per cent of the buying cycle today is carried out by buyers *before* speaking to suppliers – such is the power of the internet. Today's buyers can easily research an entire marketplace in minutes. They certainly don't need someone to connect them with products any more: they need honest advice about how to grow their business profitably and can easily tell when someone is just trying to sell them products. In short, they want to be engaged, surprised and delighted.

There are, after all, only three routes for a supplier to grow their profits:

1 Reduce or avoid costs.

2 Buy profitable businesses – limited opportunities.

3 Create demand from customers by creating value for them – the only sustainable future.

This book will show you how to quantify financially all of these and how to encapsulate them in a value proposition.

There is, however, a world of difference between merely helping your customer avoid disadvantage, and creating advantage for your customer.

Most products and services fulfil functions that customers need, in the sense that they can't do without them. For example, a restaurant needs tables and chairs; an airline needs planes; an office needs computing capability and so on. The problem, however, is that such organizations always have a choice of suppliers, and since most products today work perfectly well, they will in the main buy on price, unless a supplier can prove that they will create advantage for them. Table 1.3 shows a simple classification of this concept.

Table 1.3 Summary of value propositions

	Strategic	High potential
Creating advantage		
Avoiding disadvantage		
	Key operational	Support

Key:
Strategic: issues that will ensure the customer's long-term success.
High potential: issues that, while not crucial currently, could potentially lead to 'differential' advantage for the customer.
Key operational: issues that, unless resolved reasonably quickly, could lead to disadvantage for the customer.
Support: issues that, while of a non-urgent nature, such as information availability, nonetheless need to be solved to avoid disadvantage for the customer.

We have already explained that it is possible to succeed by financially quantifying standard benefits when other competitors don't, but this is unlikely to lead to sustainable success. The process of creating advantage for the customer, however, will lead to sustainable success.

Actions

Hopefully we have convinced you of the need for differentiation. We suggest you start by looking at your website. Is it set out in terms of the problem the customer faces, or in terms of what you offer? If the latter, you need to consider a complete overhaul of your website.

References

1 Denning, S (2011) Why did IBM survive? *Forbes*. Available at: https://www.forbes.com/sites/stevedenning/2011/07/10/why-did-ibm-survive/#1c4d795f1cac [6 June 2017].

2 Malcolm Frank, Senior Vice President, Strategy and Marketing, Cognizant, as presented at ITSMA's Marketing Leadership Forum, April 2006.

3 BBC News UK (2013) Horsemeat scandal: Withdrawn products and test results. *BBC*. Available at: http://www.bbc.co.uk/news/world-21412590 [Last accessed 23 November 2017].

Quantifying the emotional elements of value propositions

This book is principally about the first three components of a value proposition spelled out at the beginning of the next chapter. The fourth component concerns the 'emotional' elements and this chapter is devoted to this. Please read this chapter – it is important! The reason it is important is that, even if value propositions are approximately the same, it is frequently the brand or the reputation of the supplier that will win the business.

Introduction

Our aim in writing this chapter is twofold: first, it should be an enjoyable and interesting read; second, you should be able to make some significant changes to the way you deal with your markets and customers – changes that will definitely enhance your profitability.

Let us confess up front, however, that this emotional/trust element of value propositions is extremely difficult to quantify other than at an overall company level, as we will demonstrate soon.

Nonetheless, this chapter is a *must* read for all who strive to grow revenue and profits in difficult and overcrowded markets. If you implement our advice given in this chapter, you will most definitely become a lot more profitable!

There is no such thing as a 'rational' customer

The economists have a lot to answer for. Twentieth-century economics was based on the nonsensical assumption that human beings are rational. In the words of the economist, they calculate their maximum utility using perfect information to reach perfect decisions, that is, a precise point on a precise graph. We as authors, however, have never met anyone like this...

We know a millionaire who, renowned for being incredibly rational, analysed 20 different yachts before investing using a spreadsheet to assess and compare. He ended up purchasing the nineteenth option on his list. It became clear that was his preferred choice because of its image, as opposed to being the best yacht. Just a moment's thought about the world's most famous brands will, with rare exceptions, indicate that the purely functional features are not what differentiates them. More about this later in the chapter.

The truth, of course, is that emotion and attitude have always played a big part in life and will continue to do so.

Some readers will have heard of the Coca-Cola/Pepsi taste tests, which are repeated at frequent intervals. Studies such as Koenigs and Tranel in 2008 have proven that without labels, a large majority prefer the taste of Pepsi. On repeating the experiment with brand labels attached, a big majority prefer the taste of Coca-Cola, who also happen to be brand leaders. Such experiments were conducted by neurologists, comparing with respondents who have a damaged ventromedial prefrontal cortex – the part of the brain that is linked to emotion. Those in this second set abolished the 'Pepsi paradox', preferring Pepsi even when shown the labels. The conclusion was that emotion plays a major role in decision-making.[1] Therefore, even the world of medicine has proven that emotion is a big factor in decision-making.

Most importantly, this emotional element in buying has had a major impact on business and how it is valued. Take, for example, balance sheets. What they show is that while accountants don't measure intangible assets, the discrepancy between market and book values shows that investors do.

Over the past decades, buy-outs of many well-known organizations such as Rowntree by Nestlé have resulted in payments as high as five times the balance sheet value, in some cases higher. Take for example, Procter & Gamble (P&G), who paid $53.4 billion for Gillette on 1 October 2005. However, only a small proportion of this was tangible assets. P&G were then able to announce their success in a 2008 annual report that Gillette Fusion had gone from launch to billion-dollar stature in just two years, the fastest in P&G history.[2]

The problem now of course is that the new balance sheet no longer 'balances', so the error is corrected by adding a balancing figure called 'goodwill' to the assets side. While we fully understand the international accounting rules in respect of financial reports, the point we want to make is that it isn't always tangible assets that win customers; it is also the image, reputation, brands and the way a supplier deals with its customers.

After all, when Nestlé bought Rowntree, the last thing they wanted was a factory in York – they could build one of those. What they wanted and paid a premium for was their brand names, such as Kit Kat, for it was these that created profits in excess of the market average. Looking at this issue from a global perspective, it can be seen from Figure 2.1 that in the USA, tangible assets account for only 27 per cent of total corporate value, while in the UK, it is 36 per cent.

This indicates just how important it is to have offers that you can charge a premium for. The name that appears on your offers is extremely important. In fact, everything an organization does, from R&D to after-sales service, converges on the value proposition that is offered to the customer and is represented by the brand name.

Figure 2.1 Asset breakdown for the top 10 countries by enterprise value (US$ millions, 2015)

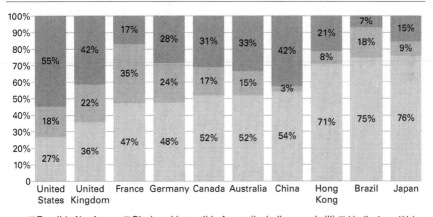

Tangible Net Assets   Disclosed Intangible Assets (including goodwill)   Undisclosed Value

Ranked by tangible net asset%

SOURCE Brand Finance plc

So what is a brand and why is it so important?

Without getting into technical definitions, let us simplify it by saying that there are three layers of branding:

1 The first is the logo and associated visual elements. But unless this logo has associated goodwill, it is just a name on a product or service. This applies to the majority of products and services.

2 The second is a broader bundle of associated intellectual property rights, such as product design rights, adverting visuals, packaging and the like. Mercedes design and the Guinness recipe and production process are good examples of this.

3 A holistic company and organization brand which, taken together, create specific value propositions and stronger customer relationships.

So, 'brand' means one of the following:

- 'trademark';
- 'brand';
- 'branded business'.

A brilliant example of a branded business and the added value it can create is shown in Figure 2.2. Forget consumer petrol, as this is an extremely minor

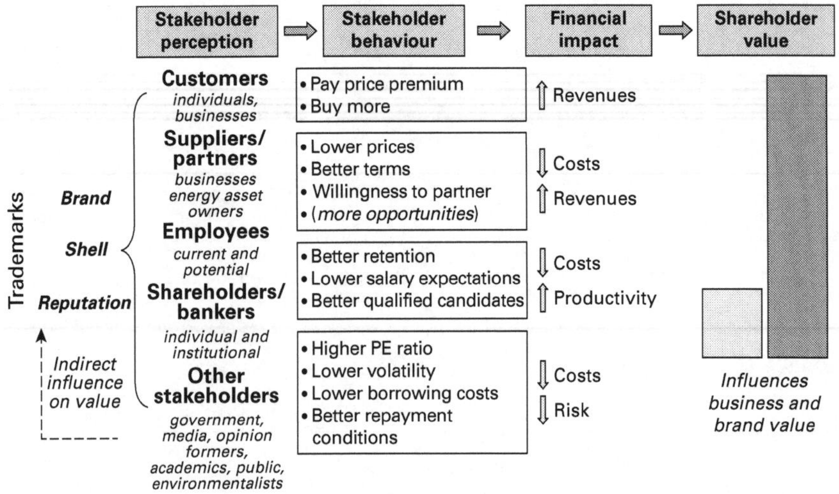

Figure 2.2   Shell: brands increasingly drive business results

part of Shell's business. In most of this business-to-business trade in most countries of the world, Shell is number one and can charge premium prices for its products. This is the value of a great brand name.

Brands affect business value by influencing the behaviour of a wide range of Shell's stakeholders, some of which directly impact Shell's profit and loss (P&L) (and hence value).

One of the quickest ways to become indistinguishable from your competitors when times are hard is to resort to cost-cutting, as we saw in Chapter 1 with the cost-cutting supermarket disasters in 2013. Excessive cost-cutting turns customers away, depressing profits and creating even greater pressure on costs.

Just look again at what unsuccessful brands do. In a sense, it's a bit like putting lipstick on a gorilla in the hope that it will look more attractive! But customers and consumers are not that easily fooled. A brand that creates sustainable premium prices and margins is extremely important. Although brands such as Coca-Cola, IBM, Microsoft, GE, Google and McDonald's are all multinationals, they give some sense of the power of intangible assets.

Brand valuation

The billion-dollar sums given in reports look precise, and while they may be very approximately right, no one has yet agreed on how to evaluate a brand other than to sell it at a market price. In 2014, *Marketing Week* quoted the 'BrandZ top 100 most valuable brands' as growing by 7 per cent to $2.6 trillion.[3]

Nonetheless, when it comes to value propositions, there is no doubt that a trusted brand has a lot of intrinsic value over and above the quantified benefits of the offer itself.

The term 'brand equity' has a financial connotation to it. It is the set of assets (and liabilities) inherent in a brand that add (or subtract) value in a firm and its customers. The term 'customer equity' is the sum of the customer lifetime values to the organization. Both represent different perspectives of the same intangible asset, as the financial worth in both cases is estimated by taking the net present values of the same future cash flows. Both create values when they create cash flows which, when discounted using net present value methods (NPV), are greater than the investment. Discounted cash flow and NPV methods have been used for well over half a century in evaluating investments and are now widely used for evaluating marketing investments such as brands. Brand valuation companies such as Brand

Finance and Interbrand have designed sophisticated methods for valuing brands, but depending on the evaluation method chosen, these often result in widely differing sums.

Nonetheless, even though brand and customer valuation are still a long way from being an exact science, the fact remains that investing in brands in particular can have a major impact on the emotional element of the purchasing decision and will almost always give you an advantage.

What remains as a problem, however, is that it is extremely difficult when quantifying value propositions to put a precise financial value on the emotional/branding element.

The key thing to remember is that everything an organization does is projected to the customer via the brand name, and the problem with not having a powerful brand name is that price will almost certainly be the only determinant of customer choice, given that most products perform more or less equally today.

Before we get into the serious business of explaining how to quantify value propositions financially, however, there is one other major determinant of commercial success. We urge you to read this next section, because without doubt it has a major impact on brand differentiation and profitable growth. We refer to market segmentation.

Market segmentation: the bedrock of profitable growth

Let us start by quoting from a *Harvard Business Review* article published in 2005: 'of 30,000 new products launched each year, 90% of them fail because of poor market segmentation.'[4] Our own unpublished research shows extremely poor levels of market segmentation competence. Over 30 years we have examined 3,000 marketing plans, of which only 500 had needs-based segmentation (16 per cent). The reasons are clear to us.

Dispelling some popular myths

First, most people think market segmentation is concerned with socio-economic demographics, geodemographics and the like. But apart from being useful as a very high level of aggregation – in the sense that, clearly, certain age groups and certain socio-economic groups will be bigger users of some types of goods and services – they do not help suppliers. Take socio-economic group A. They do not all behave the same. Just like all males between the ages of 15 and 18 do not behave the same, nor does everyone in the same street (geodemographics).

So, we must move beyond this somewhat basic notion of what market segmentation is. A market segment is a group of people with the same or similar needs and in any market there will be between five and ten such groups.

First, however, let's understand why market segmentation is so important and why it is particularly important in mature or saturated markets. Let's look again at the customer portfolio from the introduction (Figure 2.3).

You can see from this that the bulk of most markets in terms of revenue comes from the middle group – the Mr and Mrs Average customer. There are exceptions, of course, but let's ignore these for now. The 'Mr and Mrs Average' part of the market grows rapidly until the market matures, when there tends to be a surplus of supply over demand, at which point most suppliers have little option but to drop their prices as they are competing with other suppliers who offer very similar products. This, as we have seen, has a devastating impact on their profits.

Figure 2.3   The customer portfolio

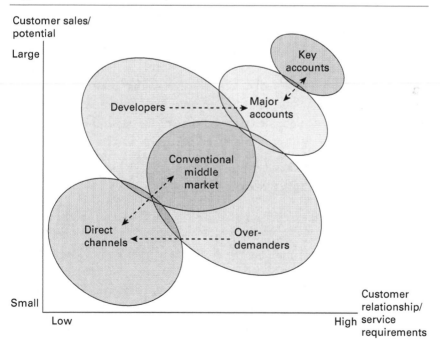

Figure 2.4   The product/market lifecycle and market characteristics

Key characteristics	Unique	Product differentiation	Service differentiation	'Commodity'
Marketing message	Explain	Competitive	Brand values	Corporate
Sales	Pioneering	Relative benefits Distribution support	Relationship based	Availability based
Distribution	Direct selling	Exclusive distribution	Mass distribution	80 : 20
Price	Very high	High	Medium	Low (consumer controlled)
Competitive intensity	None	Few	Many	Fewer, bigger International
Costs	Very high	Medium	Medium/low	Very low
Profit	Medium/high	High	Medium/high	Medium/low
Management style	Visionary	Strategic	Operational	Cost management

Look at it another way. Figure 2.4 shows what happens in most markets and we can refer to a typical example to illustrate our point. The brand 3M Post-it notes, when first introduced, were unique, prices were high and promotion was heavy. Eventually, other competitors entered the market with cheaper 'own label' versions until the market became saturated. The product is now a commodity and the market characteristics are totally different – see the far right column. 3M's product, however, is still premium priced because of clever segmentation.

The important point to make here, however, is that most suppliers only drop their prices in mature markets because they do not understand the behaviours and motivations of their customers. Those suppliers, however, like 3M, who do, continue to make handsome profits.

Proper, needs-based segmentation

The first point to make is that suppliers do not sell to organizations; they sell to *people* in organizations, and these people will inevitably fall into groups with different attitudes and behaviours, or segments.

Let's take an example based on a major player in the office supplies market, in particular their after-sales service. Their customer surveys showed an increasingly low level of satisfaction by their customers, so they carried out a proper needs-based market segment project. The results are shown here:

Koala Bears

Found in: Small offices, 28 per cent of the market (both small and big companies). Personality type: sheltered. Use an extended warranty to give them cover. Prefer to bring in outsourced support rather than use in-house resources.

Teddy Bears

Found in: Larger companies, 17 per cent of the market. Personality type: protected. Lots of account management and love required from a single preferred supplier. Will pay a premium for training and attention. If multi-site, will require supplier to effectively cover these sites.

Polar Bears

Found in: Larger companies, 29 per cent of the market. Personality type: Like teddy bears but colder! Will shop around for the cheapest service supplier, whoever that may be. Full third-party approach. Train me but don't expect to be paid. Will review annually. If multi-site, they will require supplier to effectively cover this site.

Yogi Bears

Found in: Large and small companies, 11 per cent of the market. A 'wise' Teddy or Polar Bear working long hours. Will use trained staff to fix if possible. Needs skilled product specialist at the end of the phone, not a bookings clerk. Wants different service levels to match the criticality of the product to their business process.

Grizzly Bears

Not found in: small companies, 6 per cent of market. Cheaper to replace than maintain. So reliable they often become obsolete when they bust. Expensive items will be fixed on a pay-as-when basis if worth it. Won't pay for training.

Andropov Big Bears

Not found in: small or very large companies, 9 per cent of the market. My business is totally dependent on your products. I know more about them than you do! You will be on demand and follow our direction. I will pay for the extra cover but you will do XYZ.

Without going into the details, even a cursory glance will indicate that the levels of services required by the 'Koala Bears' would be totally different from those demanded by 'Andropov Big Bears'. But until this point, the company had been providing a similar level of service across the whole market. With the market segmentation exercise, they were able to tailor their service to the needs of each segment and as a consequence turned a low-profit business into a highly profitable one.

One more example should convince you. A quick look at Table 2.1 reveals that there is no single definition of 'doctor' and any pharmaceutical company hoping to be successful would need to recognize this and behave accordingly.

Table 2.1   Segmentation example: what defines a doctor?

GP type	Characteristics
Type 1 Disillusioned 17%	Innovative in prescribing because this adds variety to a mundane job Not interested in developing professionally – 'medicine is not all it's cracked up to be' Pro-technology Distrusts the industry Would like few drug controls
Type 2 Postgraduate 21%	Formal GP Anti-promotion and avoids new drugs Strong postgraduate interests, wants to develop professionally Conservative prescriber
Type 3 Self-satisfied 19%	Satisfied as a GP Very conservative prescriber Low interest in postgraduate education 'Low-tech' doctor
Type 4 Experimentalist 12%	Innovative because they would like to try new drugs and 'experiment' Pro-promotion Has some interests in professional development
Type 5 Overstretched 12%	Formal type of GP Disillusioned with medicine – hard work, few rewards Often in single-handed inner city practices

(continued)

Table 2.1   (*Continued*)

GP type	Characteristics
	Anti-technology Low graduate interests Wants their life made easier Fairly conservative prescriber
Type 6 Progressive 19%	Informal type of GP Satisfied with their job and medicine as a profession Strong postgraduate interests Pro-technology Prepared to try new drugs

Summary so far

If you can implement needs-based segmentation in your business, you will have an enormous advantage over competitors who are still talking about their products and services, emphasizing their offers and their communications across the entire market and trying to appeal to the non-existent 'average customer'.

We hope we have convinced you to take action, as the very nature of each value proposition will vary depending on which segment it is aimed at.

By way of a summary of this section, consider the example shown in the box below. You will immediately recognize many of the emotional elements shown in the column on the following page. But not everyone has the same emotional needs, which is where segmentation becomes so important. You will also appreciate that it is rarely the physical characteristics of a product that determines who will choose to buy it and why.

Example of consumer needs when purchasing Beer

Physical needs:

- alcohol strength;
- appearance;
- pouring satisfaction;
- packaging appearance;

- shape and size;
- taste;
- colour;
- relaxation;
- stimulation.

Emotional needs:

- self-display;
- prestige;
- aspiration;
- social group identification;
- safety;
- reassurance;
- success;
- fashion;
- style;
- masculinity/femininity;
- companionship;
- distinctiveness.

Putting it into action

So now let's get you started on needs-based market segmentation – something I've laid out in a couple of my books. We need to make a crucial point about where in your business you should be doing market segmentation. Figure 2.5 shows what is commonly referred to as Pareto's law, showing that 20 per cent of all inputs will usually account for about 80 per cent of outputs.

We will refer to this again in Chapter 3.

Now, have a look at Table 2.2. All we need you to do is to discover the 20 per cent of your products, services and markets which account for 80 per cent of your sales. There shouldn't be more than five or six. Take the most important of these and try the following market segmentation exercise.

Figure 2.5   Pareto's Law

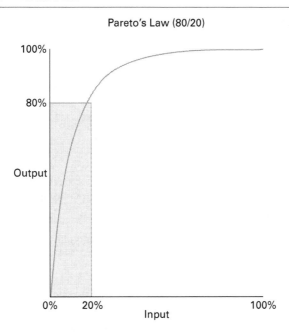

I am pleased to present the following models and extracts in this chapter from *Malcolm McDonald on Marketing Planning,* featured here based on the sheer value it will bring to your company in the context of building the basis of your quantifiable value proposition. Once finished, you'll see exactly what I mean!

SBU Product-Market table

1 Select a business unit, or part of the business, for which you wish to develop a Value Proposition unit: _____

2 Along the top of the table overleaf, list the principal products, product groups or services sold by the business unit, ignoring unimportant ones.

Table 2.2   SBU product-market table

Products: Markets:	1:	2:	3:	4:	5:
1:					
2:					
3:					
4:					
5:					

1 Down the left of the table, list the principal markets, or market segments, you sell into, ignoring unimportant ones.

2 Now choose 1 to 2 product-markets (cells) to concentrate on during this book. For each, estimate your current revenue in the box.

You are now ready to begin your market segmentation projects.

Before attempting this, however, we need to explain that it isn't quite as simple as the following exercise makes it out to be, and for those who feel the need to do it in more depth, please get hold of *Malcolm McDonald on Marketing Planning* (2016)[5] or *Market Segmentation* (2012).[6]

Exercise for generating preliminary market segments

Please follow the sequence of activities shown below and you will generate a few segments. Please note that while we do not recommend giving the resulting segments silly names, it can nonetheless be useful to make them memorable and meaningful!

Quick segmentation exercise[7]

- Write down the main benefits sought by customers.
- Divide them into:
  - hygiene factors;
  - motivators (those that contribute towards the customer's decision on who to buy from).

- Take the 'motivators' and choose the two main ones.
- Estimate the percentage of customers at each end.
- Cross-multiply them to create a perceptual map.
- Give them names.

Quick market segmentation solution

- Write down the *main* benefits sought by customers.
- Hygiene factors are benefits that any product or service must have to be acceptable in the market. Try to ignore these.
- Motivators are those benefits that contribute towards the customer's decision about which product to buy.
- Take the 'motivators' and choose the two main ones.
- Draw two straight horizontal lines and make an estimate of the percentage of customers at each end. So, for example, if service level is a key motivator of what is bought, see below:

40% ————————————— 60%	
Low service	High service

- Likewise, if the breadth of the product range is a key motivator of what is bought, see below:

40% ————————————— 60%	
Low range	High range

- Take the left-hand point of the first horizontal line and drag it over the second horizontal line to make a cross, as shown in Figure 2.6.
- Starting at the top, and moving in a clockwise direction, multiply 60 per cent by 60 per cent to give 36 per cent (see first circle).
- Then multiply 60 per cent by 40 per cent to give 24 per cent (see second circle).
- Then multiply 40 per cent (the bottom of the vertical axis) by 40 per cent to give 16 per cent (see fourth circle).
- The circles represent segments in the market.

Figure 2.6 Resulting matrix of quick segmentation exercise

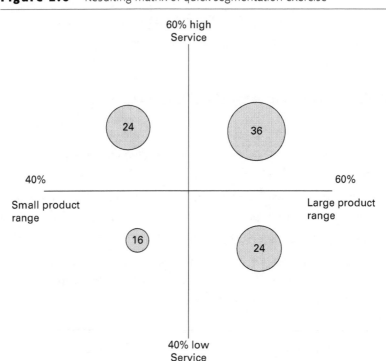

Interpretation

- The first segment (36 per cent), the biggest segment, requires both high service and a large product range.

- The second segment (24 per cent) prefers a large product range and is less interested in service.

- The third segment (16 per cent) doesn't care much about either a large product range or service.

- The fourth segment (24 per cent) prefers good service and is less interested in a large product range.

- Although not essential, you might consider giving each segment a name.

Action

Ensure your 'offer', including the product, price, service and promotion, reflect the differing needs of each segment.

Example

An example of segmentation of the A4 paper market follows. Please note that if, as in the case of the A4 paper market, there is one very large segment (in this case 56 per cent), the exercise can be repeated for just this large segment, resulting in seven segments in total.

Example = copier paper

- Service delivery: fast, paper always 'there' – point-of-delivery availability of products; service levels.

- Product fit for purpose: high-quality print finish for colour copiers; consistency of quality; paper that doesn't screw up in the machine; print definition; no waste.

- Environmental factors: recyclable.

- Level of support: delivered in small lots; consignment stock; easy ordering (online); delivered to difficult locations.

Figure 2.7 Example of quick segmentation exercise: copier paper

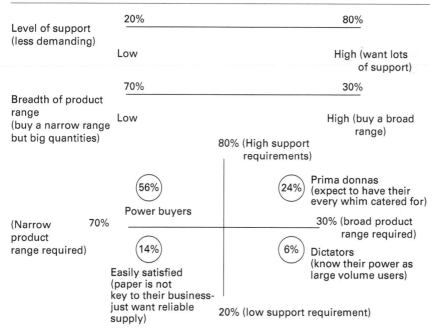

Table 2.3   A summary of the problems facing many companies today and the answers

Problem	Falling demand	Falling prices	Falling profits
Answer	Proper segmentation	Superior value Different positioning	Rising profits

You will generate from this exercise four segments, but usually one is much bigger than the others, so take the biggest and do the exercise again from the beginning, generating two new sets of buying motivators. You will now generate another four segments, making seven in total.

Finally

In conclusion, we want to make two points:

1 Implementing proper needs-based segmentation will give you significant competitive advantage.

2 In preparing financially quantified value propositions, there are several levels at which these apply. The highest level is at a company or strategic business unit level. The next level is at a product group level. Then there is the individual product or service level.

All of this should be considered in the context of segments, as each segment, as illustrated above, has a different emphasis based on a different set of needs and attitudes.

Actions

Use the segmentation exercise described above to generate seven segments.

References

1   Koenigs, M and Tranel, D (2008) 'Prefrontal cortex damage abolishes brand-cued preference', SCAN 3, pp 2–6, Department of Neurology, University of Iowa College of Medicine. https://www.ncbi.nlm.nih.gov/pmc/articles/PMC2288573/

2 P&G (2008) *Designed to innovate: 2008 annual report*. P&G. Available at page 29: https://www.pg.com/annualreport2008/PG_2008_AnnualReport.pdf [Last accessed 23 November 2017].

3 Cooper, L (2013) The top 100 most valuable global brands 2013. *Marketing Week*. Available at: https://www.marketingweek.com/2013/05/21/the-top-100-most-valuable-global-brands-2013/ [Last accessed 23 November 2017].

4 Christensen, C, Cook, S and Hall, T (December 2005) Marketing malpractice, *Harvard Business Review*, pp 74–78.

5 McDonald, M (2016) *Malcolm McDonald on Marketing Planning*, Kogan Page, London.

6 McDonald, M and Dunbar, I (2012) *Market Segmentation*, 4th edition, John Wiley & Sons, Chichester.

7 Methodology developed by Professor Brian Smith of Pragmedic, based on Hertzberg's two-factor theory of motivation. Used here with his kind permission.

What exactly is a financially quantified value proposition?

Introduction

Below is a summary of the components of a value proposition. In this chapter we will explain each of the first three elements. The fourth element – the emotional contribution – was dealt with in Chapter 2. First, however, we need to clarify what the word 'value' means because it has numerous well-accepted interpretations.

The components of a value proposition

1 added value (eg revenue gains, improved productivity, service enhancement, speed, etc);
2 cost reduction;
3 cost avoidance;
4 emotional contribution (eg trust, 'feel-good' factor), confidence, self-esteem, risk reduction, reduced 'hassle', etc. In this respect, powerful branding is important. Effective, needs-based market segmentation is even more important.

Figure 3.1 shows examples of added value categories and the following lists the value chain benefits. We referred to emotional benefits in Chapter 2. These emotional elements of value are rooted in psychology. All readers will be aware of the widely accepted Abraham Maslow's psychology of needs, from which it can be seen that once basic functional needs are satisfied, people look for less rational sources of satisfaction.

Figure 3.1 Examples of added value categories

- Enhanced product line
- Better product mix
- Better customer mix

- More sales calls
- Better sales calls
- Price increase
- Revenue gains
- Service enhancement

- Speed
- Reduction of discounts
- Charging for deliveries
- Reduction of debtor days

- Increased closure rate
- Reduction of the sales cycle
- Avoidance of no/delayed decisions to buy

- Referrals from satisfied customers
- Sustained customer relationships

Examples of value chain cost benefits

- design and development;
- hard cash (eg labour, assets);
- operating costs (eg energy, maintenance);
- soft costs (eg overheads, training);
- installation and commission costs;
- governance costs (eg cost to manage the relationship);
- software costs;
- supply chain costs;
- retirement, disposal or residual value costs;
- opportunity costs (eg reduces downtime, increasing production yield, sales value/margin increase);
- transaction costs (eg switching supplier);
- environmental /sustainability costs.

Understanding the real meaning of customer value

Understanding more about value propositions will help make strategic marketing plans much more powerful. First, however, it is necessary to define the meaning of customer value in the context of the word 'value'. The very word is highly subjective, because it totally depends on whose point of view is being taken and the context in which the word is used.

Value chain analysis

One of the most widely used tools in business is Michael Porter's value chain analysis (1980),[1] which describes how value is created through all the functions and processes of organizations. This is fundamental to our process of value creation and will be extensively used later in this book. This is broken down between support activities and primary activities that contribute to overall margin.

Support activities include:

- firm infrastructure;
- human resource management;
- technology development;
- procurement.

Primary activities include:

- inbound logistics;
- operations;
- outbound logistics;
- marketing and sales;
- service.

Another widely used process is known as shareholder value added (SVA), first proposed by Alfred Rappaport in 1986.[2] Today it is better known as economic value added, which is risk-adjusted net free cash flows in the context of the cost of capital. If these are positive, EVA is created.

Without doubt, EVA has been one of the most widely accepted and used financial measurements of success over the past 30 years and we recommend that readers try to understand the fundamentals of how it works and is used. It calculates net free cash flows, having taken account of the time value of money, the cost of capital and the risks associated with the investment in question. The formula is:

profit after tax minus (net capital x cost of capital (%))

For readers in small or mid-sized companies, a simple example should suffice. Imagine you have £2 million of assets and your cost of capital is, say, 10 per cent. If you make £150,000 profit, you have destroyed £50,000 of value. If you make £250,000, you have created £50,000 of value. Why would any sane person run a business to destroy shareholder value?

The reason EVA is so pivotal and powerful is that it is the ultimate proof of commercial success, so if readers can move just this one step beyond financially quantified value propositions, directors and senior managers in the customer's business will be truly convinced that you are beyond doubt the best supplier to deal with. So we will return to this in Chapter 8.

Then there is the accountant's definition of value added:

value added = sales revenue – purchases and services

As discussed in my recent *Marketing Planning* book, this will provide a snapshot picture from the annual accounts of how the revenue from a sales period has been distributed, and how much is left over for reinvestment after meeting all costs, including shareholder dividends. Although this figure will say something about the past viability of a business, in itself it does not provide a guide to future prospects.

Part of the reason the term 'value added' has become used more carelessly is because these concepts of value are not mutually exclusive, despite their differences. For example, Porter's value chain analysis identifies potential new competitive market strategies, whereas Rappaport's SVA approach enables managers to cost out the long-term financial implications of pursuing competitive strategies. Whichever is used, it is the customer perception that acts as the main driver (or incumbent) of annual audited accounting value in all companies.

Customer value

A third way of looking at value is through the eyes of the customer. 'Brand equity' and 'customer equity' are financial terms to reflect the fact that brands and customers are financial assets that are capable of creating shareholder value, but the term 'customer value' is much harder to pin down, as value is an interactive, relative, preference experience. It is interactive because there is always a connection between the offer and the customer. It is relative in that the customer appraises the offer in comparison with other offers and is context dependent and personal, according to different preference criteria. For example, an offer of a seat at an Arsenal football match in the UK would be more highly valued by an Arsenal fan than by a Manchester United fan. First, value arises from a customer's consumption experience rather than being embedded in the product. This is often referred to as 'value in use', and it is therefore the customer, not the supplier, who is the ultimate arbiter of value.

Before defining the expression 'value proposition', there is one other concept that needs to be explained – 'value co-creation'. As the term implies, value is best created by the joint efforts of both the supplier and the customer. It is the degree to which the supplier works with the customer to craft an offer in such a way that benefits are translated into monetary terms based on an in-depth understanding of the customer's business, thereby demonstrating their contribution to the customer's profitability. This usually involves identifying needs and opportunities for value creation.

Our own definition of organization value co-creation is that it is an opportunity-identifying process leading to the creation of new value for all participating parties through the integration and interaction of resources. Many readers will immediately recognize this as best practice key account management, with the results embedded in a key account plan.

Alas, the actual financially quantified value proposition is frequently missing from such plans. This book is intended to fill this gap, and all that remains now is to define the term value proposition.

Value proposition

For the purpose of this book, the authors summarize this as 'relative value = perceived benefits minus costs'. As a brief reminder, we repeat here the key components, ready to tackle each of the first three points.

The components of a value proposition

1 added value (eg revenue gains, improved productivity, service enhancement, speed, etc);
2 cost reduction;
3 cost avoidance;
4 emotional contribution (eg trust, 'feel-good' factor), confidence, self-esteem, risk reduction, reduced 'hassle', etc. In this respect, powerful branding is important. Effective, needs-based market segmentation is even more important.

1 Added value

Some examples of added value categories were given earlier, but there are many ways a supplier can add value to their customers' business. The list is too long and complex to set out here, but a comprehensive example is outlined below in relation to an information systems/information technology supplier, with detailed use of Porter's value chain as an analysis tool to delve into every aspect of a customer's business from beginning to end.

Support activities:

- Firm infrastructure:
  - web-based, distributed financial and enterprise resource planning (ERP) systems;
  - online investor relations (eg information dissemination, broadcast conference call);
  - accounting systems.
- Human resource management:
  - self-service personnel and benefits administration;
  - web-based training;
  - electronic time and expense reporting.
- Technology development:
  - collaborative product design across locations and among multiple value-system participants;
  - knowledge directories accessible from all parts of the organization.
- Procurement:
  - internet-enabled demand planning; real-time available-to-promise/capable-to-promise and fulfilment;
  - other linkage of purchase, inventory and forecasting systems with suppliers;
  - direct and indirect procurement via marketplaces, exchanges, auctions, and buyer–seller matching.

Primary activities:

- Inbound logistics (web-distributed supply chain management):
  - real-time integrated scheduling, shipping, warehouse management, demand management and planning, and advanced planning and scheduling across the company and its suppliers;

- dissemination throughout the company of real-time inbound and in-progress inventory data.

- Operations (web-distributed supply chain management):
  - integrated information exchange, scheduling, and decision-making in in-house plants, contract assemblers and components suppliers;
  - real-time available-to-promise and capable-to-promise information available to the sales force and channels.

- Outbound logistics (web-distributed supply chain management):
  - real-time transaction of orders whether initiated by an end consumer, a sales person or a channel partner;
  - automated customer-specific agreements and contract terms;
  - customer and channel access to product development and delivery status;
  - collaborative integration with customer forecasting systems.

- Marketing and sales:
  - online sales channels including websites and marketplaces;
  - real-time inside and outside access to customer information, product catalogues, dynamic pricing, inventory availability, online submission of quotes and order entry;
  - online product configurators;
  - customer-tailored marketing via customer profiling;
  - push advertising;
  - tailored online access.

- After-sales service:
  - online support of customer service;
  - representatives through email response management, billing integration;
  - co-browse, chat, 'call me now', voiceover;
  - IP and other uses of video streaming.

We included a partial list in Chapter 2 on pricing and it is worth revisiting some of it here.

2 Cost reduction and cost avoidance

Cost reduction and cost avoidance are perhaps the easiest to quantify financially. We revert back to SKF, shown in Figure 3.2, a classic example of

Figure 3.2 Example of quantified value proposition – SKF

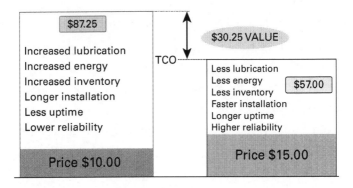

SOURCE Reproduced with kind permission of SKF, who presented the diagram at Cranfield University's KAM Best Practice Research Club in January 2015

Figure 3.3 SKF – technical benefits to customers

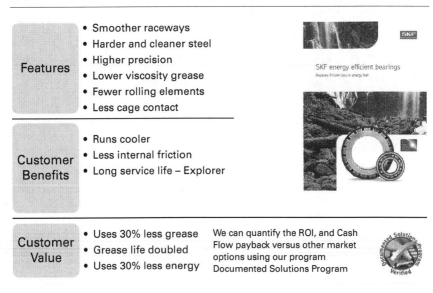

how to charge a high price up front by justifying a significant reduction in lifetime costs.

Figures 3.3 and 3.4 are examples of the kind of in-depth analysis that goes into the financially quantified value propositions of SKF.

This process works just as well for small companies, as can be seen from the example of the label company given below:

Figure 3.4 SKF – example

Spend minutes. Save thousands.   SKF

SKF Documented Solutions

SKF Y-units food line (Marathon)

The food and beverage market offers enormous growth potential, being one of the largest manufacturing and distribution sector segments in the economy. The processed food market itself grows almost at 10% per year, and has been growing at this rate for the past 25 years. The reasons of such a growth? An increased per capita income, lifestyle changes and technological innovations made necessary by world food safety trends. SKF has decided to apply its know-how, quality standards and research results on materials and technologies to create a wide range of high quality solutions in this demanding market. The result is a line of products that combines high resistance, advanced technology and extended service life.

Documented value	
Description	**Value**
Value added over MTBR (8.00 Months)	37657.45 $
Expected ROI over MTBR	390.23 %
Cash flow break-even	2.43 Months
Break-even MTBR increase percentage necessary	142.79 %
Break-even MTBR increase in months necessary	1.43 Months

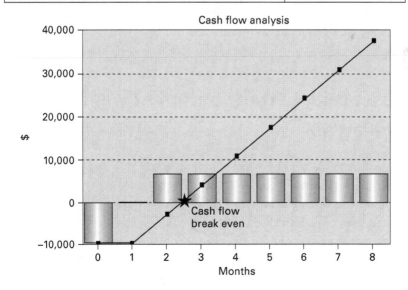

Example: label company to food manufacturers taking over responsibility for almost eliminating their stock-holding

All were quantified and tailored to each customer:

- It reduces your inventory from 6 to 12 weeks.
- It reduces the cash tied up in inventory.
- It reduces the problems when you have a stock-out.
- It reduced stock-out costs (down-time, expedited shipping, overtime).
- It reduces inventory-carrying costs.
- It reduces inventory obsolescence.
- It increases sales when you can make quick changes.
- It eliminates the need to place orders.
- And all at the same price.

Advantages to the label company:

- They answer the question: 'why should I buy from you?'
- They are different from their competitors.
- They reduce the risk of losing a customer to a competitor offering a price reduction.
- They make it more difficult for a customer to leave.
- They become better at the production and distribution processes.
- They can then gain new customers.
- Their sales and profits increase.

The emotional contribution of value propositions

We devoted the whole of Chapter 2 to this topic and we hope you read it carefully and now understand the crucial importance that a powerful brand can play in creating perceptions of value for the customer. At the very least, all things being equal in benefit terms and price, most customers will opt for a brand that they know and trust. The two of us as authors have just won a major contract for a market segmentation project and the client informed us that most bids were about equal, but what swayed the decision for the client was our widely recognized reputation for world-class market segmentation, represented by the brand name 'Malcolm McDonald'. So, even though by any standards we are a small company, branding and reputation are key to a perception in the customer's mind of risk reduction.

Conclusion

We hope we have given you a comprehensive understanding of what a financially qualified value proposition is. This was essential before explaining the process you will use to prepare them, which is what Chapter 4 is about.

Actions

Even at this preliminary stage, have a go at listing and quantifying (preferably financially), customer benefits under the first three bullet points in the opening 'components of a value proposition' box.

References

1 Porter, M (1980) *Competitive Strategy*, Free Press, New York.

2 Rappaport, A (1986) *Creating Shareholder Value*, Free Press, New York.

An overview of the value proposition process – where to start

04

Introduction

You will be pleased to know that this is a short chapter! Let us first of all set out the value proposition process, shown in Figure 4.1.

Before we take you through this, however, we must stress that the preparation of value propositions needs to be done in the context of your organization's planning processes. In other words, it has to fit into some kind of rational process in order for it to be really effective.

So, we will leave the process set out in Figure 4.1 for now and will turn to two strategic planning processes: strategic marketing planning and key account planning.

Strategic marketing planning

Figure 4.2 illustrates the strategic marketing planning process, with the emphasis being on the output of the process – the strategic marketing plan itself (in the top right box in the figure) is the document that will spell out your key target markets, why customers should buy from you rather than from someone with something similar, and with what financial results.

It is not necessary here to go through the processes from beginning to end. What is essential, however, is to note that steps 3 and 4 are about understanding market/segment needs, particularly step 4 – the SWOT analysis. So, first of all, let me explain what a SWOT analysis is and is not.

Figure 4.1   Value proposition process

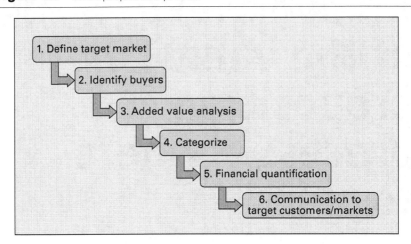

Figure 4.2   The 10 steps of the strategic marketing planning process

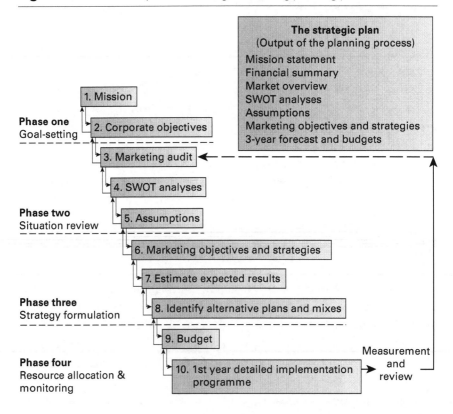

SWOT analyses

A strengths, weaknesses, opportunities and threats analysis is one of the main means of summarizing the needs of customers. In Chapter 10 we will explain in more detail how this works. For now, let us assume that a proper SWOT analysis has been conducted and that we have a pretty good understanding of the needs of customers in a particular segment.

This is where the problems of inadequate marketing really begin, because the planning process now moves directly to setting marketing objectives and strategies and doesn't bother with the crucial step of quantifying value propositions for each segment.

The main point is that it is at this stage of the planning process that financially quantified value propositions should be prepared for each segment. As we have said earlier, it is crucial to understand that value proposition preparation needs to be part of a wider strategic planning process.

> For a full explanation of these two concepts, see *Malcolm McDonald on Marketing Planning* (Kogan Page, 2016) and *Malcolm McDonald on Key Account Planning* (Kogan Page, 2017).

Figure 4.3 KAM analysis and strategy development process

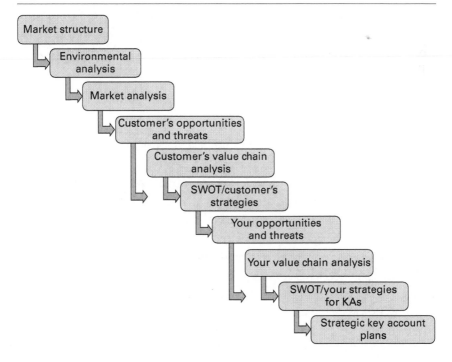

It is this lack of focus on value proposition preparation that has led to the increasing isolation of marketing from the real world of customers and to the growing feeling that marketing as a discipline has somehow lost the plot. So now let's turn to the key account management (KAM) planning process, spelled out in Figure 4.3.

The same problem that we outline above in relation to marketing planning applies to KAM planning. We will look more closely at key account (KA) needs in Chapter 8, but for now, let us focus on the penultimate step in Figure 4.3, 'your strategies for KAs'. Typically, having gone to a lot of trouble and hard work to analyse the needs of KAs, the crucial step of preparing financially quantified value propositions for them is missing. It is at this point that this book kicks in, for without them, it is less likely that the plan will be believed by the customer.

Putting the value proposition process in the context of marketing and KA planning process

Figures 4.4 and 4.5 illustrate how and where the value proposition process fits in with the marketing and KA planning process. We can now proceed to the value proposition process, reproduced in Figure 4.6.

From this it will be seen that there are a number of steps, starting with 'define target market'. In this chapter we talk you through steps 1 and 2 only and will cover steps 3, 4 and 5 in later chapters.

Define target market

This is obviously a crucial step because it defines the scope of subsequent work. There are several potential levels for developing value propositions, starting with a major customer. Another is a segment (see Chapter 2). Another is a product for a segment. At a higher level of aggregation is a product or product group for a market. The ultimate level of aggregation is for a strategic business unit (SBU) or for the entire company. This latter one may be more appropriate for small companies.

For the purpose of this book, however, we will start at a lower level of aggregation and plan for a product for a segment, or for a product for a major customer.

Figure 4.4 The 10 steps of the strategic marketing planning process

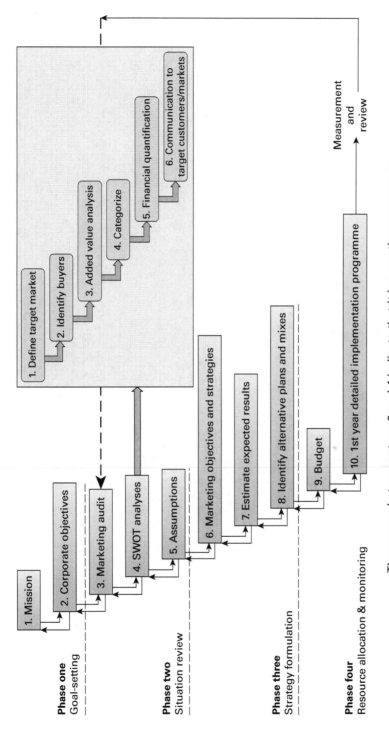

Phase one
Goal-setting

1. Mission

2. Corporate objectives

Phase two
Situation review

3. Marketing audit

4. SWOT analyses

5. Assumptions

6. Marketing objectives and strategies

7. Estimate expected results

Phase three
Strategy formulation

8. Identify alternative plans and mixes

Phase four
Resource allocation & monitoring

9. Budget

10. 1st year detailed implementation programme

1. Define target market

2. Identify buyers

3. Added value analysis

4. Categorize

5. Financial quantification

6. Communication to target customers/markets

Measurement
and
review

The arrows between steps 3 and 4 indicate that it is a continuous process

Figure 4.5 KAM analysis and strategy development process

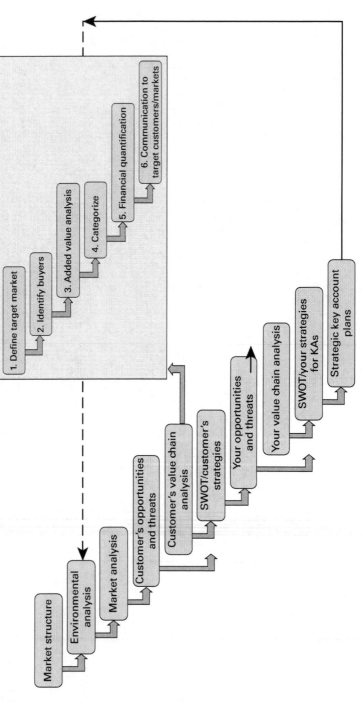

The arrow back to environmental analysis indicates that it is a continuous process

Figure 4.6   Value proposition process

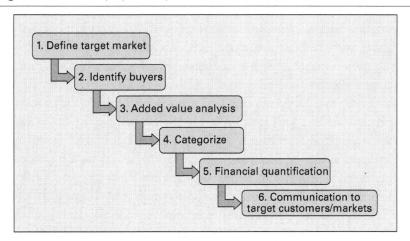

Where to begin

This first step is to decide exactly who it is that you are planning to develop value propositions for. In our experience, a good starting point is shown in Figure 4.7.

SBU Product-Market table

1 Select a business unit, or part of the business, for which you wish to develop a value proposition unit: _____

2 Along the top of Table 4.1, list the principal products, product groups or services sold by the business unit, ignoring unimportant ones.

3 Down the left of the table, list the principal markets, or market segments, you sell into, ignoring unimportant ones.

4 Now choose one to two product-markets (cells) to concentrate on during this book. For each, estimate your current revenue in the box.

Table 4.1   Product-market table

Products: Markets:	1:	2:	3:	4:	5:
1:					
2:					
3:					
4:					
5:					

As we said in Chapter 2, the first thing that completing the exercise will reveal is that approximately 80 per cent of your revenue comes from 20 per cent of your markets (or customers). We suggest that you select one of those 'boxes' to work on for the rest of this book. To refine it even more tightly, we suggest you focus on either one segment in the selected box, or on one major customer.

Taking the first of them – that is, a major product or product group for a segment – the first activity is to draw a marketing map showing how the market works from end to end.

Figure 4.7 shows a completed market map for airline seats. From this it can be seen that 40 per cent of decisions are made by large corporates and 35 per cent are made by department heads. Both of these decision points, therefore, need value propositions to be developed for them. Figure 4.8 is a template for you to develop a market map for your organization.

The purpose of all of this, of course, is to identify the decision-makers in the market, because it is the needs of these people that must be understood.

With key accounts, a different process is necessary, because it is rarely one person – the 'buyer' – who makes the decision about what to buy. Figure 4.9 shows the decision-making steps on the left, the people and company departments that might be involved along the top, and some possible pieces of information each may need along the bottom. We will explain this in more detail in Chapters 5 and 8. For now, all that is necessary is to understand that even in key accounts, it is *people* who buy and you will need to adjust your value propositions to appeal to the needs and interests of those who make or influence the decision about what is bought. Although this reference is dated 1967, it has proven over the years to be a brilliant method for deciding what information needs to be communicated to which people during the sales process.

We need to make one final point about market maps. Many organizations, such as SKF, rarely trade directly with customers. They reach the market through intermediaries such as distributors. In some cases, market maps are quite complicated, so it is crucial to understand where the important decision points are in the value chain.

We now move on to explore how customers buy.

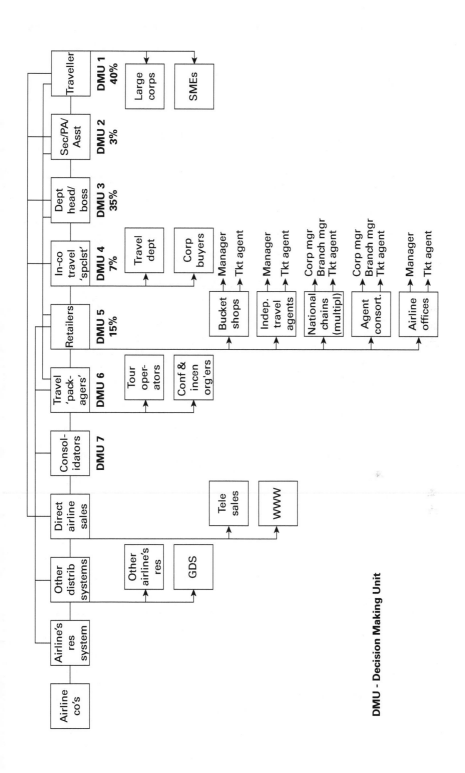

DMU - Decision Making Unit

Figure 4.8   Market map – complete for your business to define decision points

Figure 4.9   Customer buying analysis form

Customer Analysis Form	Customer _____
Salesperson _____	Address _____
Products _____	_____ Telephone number _____
_____	Buy class new buy straight re-buy modified re-buy
Date of analysis _____	
Date of reviews _____	_____ _____ _____ _____

Member of Decision Making Unit (DMU)	Production	Sales & Marketing	Research & Development	Finance & Accounts	Purchasing	Data Processing	Other
Buy Phase Name							
1 Recognizes need or problem and works out general solution							
2 Works out characteristics and quantity of what is needed							
3 Prepares detailed specification							
4 Searches for and locates potential sources of supply							
5 Analyses and evaluates tenders, plans, products							
6 Selects supplier							
7 Places order							
8 Checks and tests products							

Factors for consideration	1 price 2 performance 3 availability	4 back-up service 5 reliability of supplier 6 other users' experience	7 guarantees and warranties 8 payment terms, credit or discount 9 other, eg. past purchases, prestige, image, etc.

SOURCE Adapted from J. Robinson, C.W. Farris and Y. Wind, *Industrial Buying and Creative Marketing*, Allyn and Bacon

Actions

1 Decide where you are going to focus your value development process.

2 Complete a market map for your business to locate who the decision-makers are.

Why it is critical 05
to understand
how key buying
decisions are made

This chapter is set out in two sections: first, how major customers buy; and second, how other customers buy.

1 How major customers buy

Introduction

Why are customers today so powerful? Arguably, the business world in the 1950s and 1960s was fairly complacent. Markets had been growing and it is easy to succeed in growth markets. The 1970s brought the shock of the oil crisis and the growth of information technology. By the mid-1980s, the globalization of business offered purchasing professionals a whole new world of potential sources of supply and opportunities to dramatically reduce their cost base. During the years of 1990 and 2008, there were a number of economic traumas, the worst being the global recession of 2007/08. This gave buyers an unprecedented opportunity to apply pressure to their suppliers. The reality, of course, is that if you can buy 'stuff' from a host of suppliers – and given that most are undifferentiated – the obvious strategy for buyers is to choose their suppliers on price alone.

Figure 5.1 is a simple illustration of the impact of reduction in costs a supplier can have on the customer's net profits.

Obviously buyers had to manage risk as well, and as their skills developed to take on the new strategic role of purchasing, they needed suppliers who could accompany them on the journey.

Figure 5.1   Double your money: cut spend on purchases

Other costs (44%)

Purchases (50%)

Profit (6%)

Other costs 44%

Purchases (45%)

Profit (11%)

SOURCE 'Purchasing: adding value to your purchasing through effective supply management', Institute of Directors, September 2003

In fact, purchasing decisions-makers were demanding a change from the opportunistic selling developed over previous decades. They wanted to discuss their finances, their business processes, their organization and their culture. They wanted suppliers who could offer them routes to competitive advantage, not just products.

Figure 5.2   Increasing costs of interfacing with customers[1]

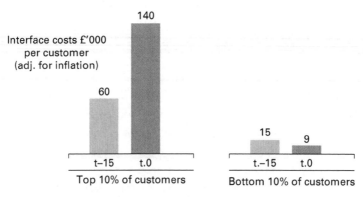

Costs of the front line (Sales, service, trade promotions etc over 15 years)

140

Interface costs £'000 per customer (adj. for inflation)

60

t–15   t.0
Top 10% of customers

15
9

t.–15   t.0
Bottom 10% of customers

Supplier to the print industry (turnover £200M)

SOURCE *Profitable Customers*, by Charles Wilson

Figure 5.3   Increasing customer concentration

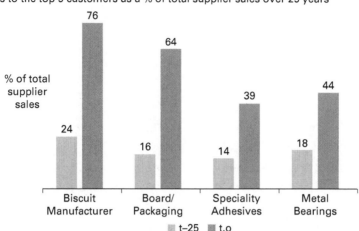

Sales to the top 5 customers as a % of total supplier sales over 25 years

Most suppliers were incapable of taking on this new mindset and different behaviours. The result was the approach from customers shown in Figure 5.1, which in turn led to reduced supplier margins and increased costs, as illustrated in Figure 5.2.

In many industries, there has been a growing trend to see a small number of global leaders and this has led in turn to the development of the key account management domain.

The result of all of this has been a dramatic shift in the balance of power from suppliers to customers, so it is important to understand how customers buy and what they consider to be important.

The need to define who the customer is

The following box illustrates the importance of understanding who the customer is. It is a summary of a conversation between the authors and one of our clients.

Case study insight: clarifying a key customer's identity[2]

Below is a hypothetical discussion about the identity of a customer at the beginning of a customer selection workshop:

  'So which key customer are we talking about here?'

  'Nokia'

> *'Is that all of Nokia?'*
>
> *'Yes'*
>
> *'All of Nokia, including televisions, mobile phones and any other divisions?'*
>
> *'Oh no, not all that, it's the mobile phone division. Our sister companies deal with the rest.'*
>
> *'So it's all of Nokia mobile phones, worldwide?'*
>
> *'No, because we only deal with Western Europe. We have SBUs in Asia Pacific and the Americas which deal with those areas.'*
>
> *'OK, so the customer as far as you are concerned is actually all the SBUs of Nokia mobile phones that buy in Western Europe?'*
>
> *'Yes.'*

Figure 5.4 illustrates another frequent misunderstanding on the part of suppliers about their power. It shows the mistaken belief that they have 100 per cent of the available wallet, whereas the customer looked at the supplier in a different light and knew that this particular supplier had only 17 per cent of the available wallet, or at best, 29 per cent.

The need to understand who 'the buyer' is

Figures 5.5 and 5.6 illustrate the complexity of a supplier with many separate product groups or business groups dealing with a customer with many product

Figure 5.4   Defining the customer's 'wallet'

How does the customer view the spend?

Purchases	Share of wallet
Incontinence pads £100k	100%
Over the counter (OTC) incontinence products £250k	40%
All incontinence products (OTC & ethical) £350k	29%
All products for the elderly £600k	17%

Check the purchase budget group

Figure 5.5   Considering the customer's structure[3]

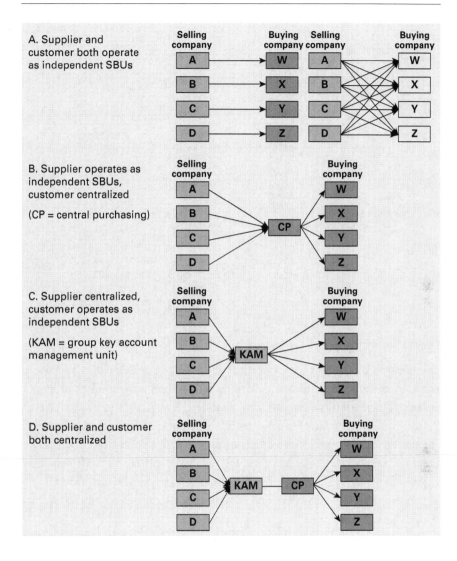

groups or business groups. Clearly, the most effective way of doing business is the structure at the bottom of each figure. The supplying company, however, needs to be aware of the additional power that the customer has if they centralize their buying, while the supplier continues to sell in a decentralized way.

The notion of 'the buyer', however, is also intensely misleading. We will deal later in this chapter with those who are purchasing professionals, as they are extremely important and frequently are the ones who make the final decision. Nonetheless, purchasing professionals, or 'buyers' as we will

Figure 5.6   Case study: DHL & manufacturers

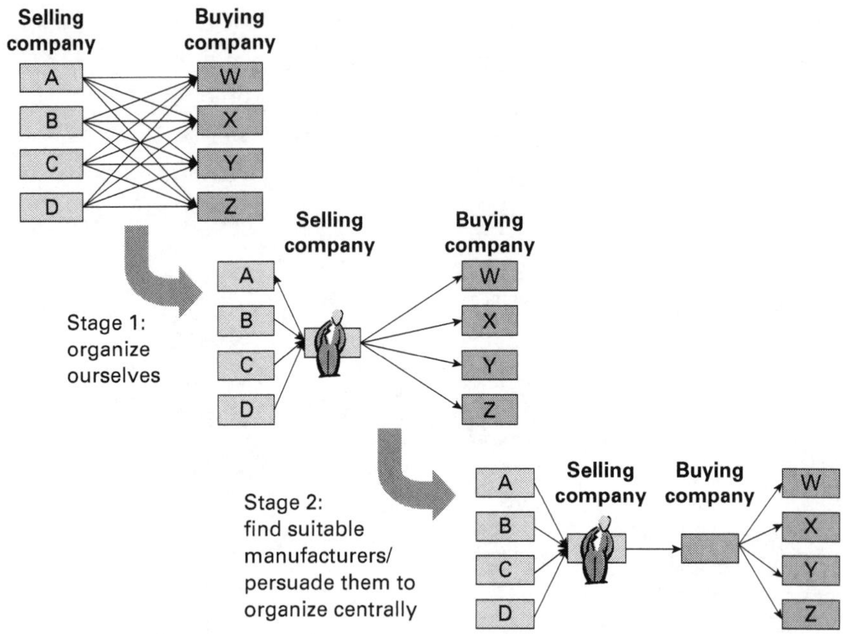

call them in this chapter, have been trained to take account of the views of those in their organization who will either use the purchased products or services or who will be impacted by them.

At this point we can revisit the template in Figure 5.7, an abiding method for understanding who these other influencers are and understanding their business decisions. This shows down the left-hand side a well-respected eight-step process that many organizations go through when they are buying expensive goods and services. The steps are simpler if it is a modified re-buy or a straight re-buy.

It is now possible for the supplying company, having identified the relevant influencers and their needs, to ensure that they get the right information to the right people *before* the buyer makes the decision about which supplier to do business with.

This reminds us of a sales workshop we ran for a components manufacturer in Australia. They had bid for – but failed to win – a multi-million-dollar deal with a Japanese car manufacturer. We asked them to complete the data in Figure 5.7 and, after its completion, they admitted that they had managed to get only 30 per cent of the right information to the right people. They consequently agreed that in future they would do this analysis for all major sales.

Figure 5.7 Customer analysis form

Customer Analysis Form	Customer _____
Salesperson _____	Address _____
Products _____	_____ Telephone number _____
_____	Buy class new buy straight re-buy modified re-buy
Date of analysis _____	
Date of reviews _____ _____ _____ _____ _____	

Member of Decision Making Unit (DMU)	Production	Sales & Marketing	Research & Development	Finance & Accounts	Purchasing	Data Processing	Other
Buy Phase Name							
1 Recognizes need or problem and works out general solution							
2 Works out characteristics and quantity of what is needed							
3 Prepares detailed specification							
4 Searches for and locates potential sources of supply							
5 Analyses and evaluates tenders, plans, products							
6 Selects supplier			·				
7 Places order							
8 Checks and tests products							

Factors for consideration	1 price 2 performance 3 availability	4 back-up service 5 reliability of supplier 6 other users' experience	7 guarantees and warranties 8 payment terms, credit or discount 9 other, eg. past purchases, prestige, image, etc.

One of the major potential benefits of this kind of approach can be seen from Figure 5.9. Here, it will be observed that any supplier successfully getting into contact early in the sales cycle will have a major advantage as the sales process nears completion, as it is at this stage that most of the costs of bidding, etc, are incurred for bidders entering much later.

There are two types of buying professional

Figure 5.9 illustrates the new buyer's interest in the value chain. It shows that most buyers today are interested in buying goods and services that will help their organizations reduce costs, avoid costs, or add value to their offers to their own customers. We have no data to support the assertion that most professional buyers are like this and we still see lots of evidence that there are plenty of old-fashioned buyers whose only goal is to reduce supplier costs. Indeed, we were addressing a conference of professional buyers in Geneva and established that less than 50 per cent were paid to win additional value for their organizations as opposed to being paid to get prices down. The encouraging fact to emerge, however, was that a big majority knew that buying on value-in-use would be their preferred way of buying.

The disastrous consequences of buying only on price can be seen in the many huge government contracts, most of which have been a disaster and which subsequently cost the taxpayer dearly.

Figure 5.8 Supplier advantage by contact early in the sales cycle

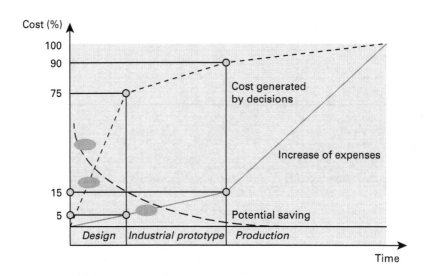

Figure 5.9 The supply chain – new buyer's interest

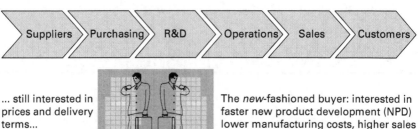

... still interested in prices and delivery terms...

The *new*-fashioned buyer: interested in faster new product development (NPD) lower manufacturing costs, higher sales values, and satisfied customers.

Figure 5.10 Spend mapping 1

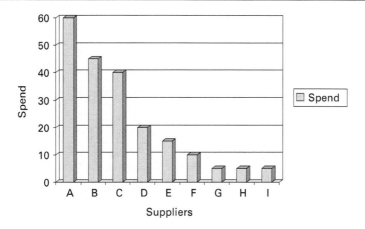

Short case history of the very worst kind of buyer

Figure 5.10 illustrates the situation a buying director of a key account might inherit when taking a job on. This case history is based on a presentation this particular buyer gave to a large audience of key account managers. From Figure 5.10 it can be seen that there were nine suppliers, the biggest

Figure 5.11 Spend mapping 2

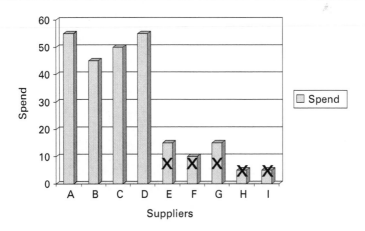

Figure 5.12   Spend mapping 3

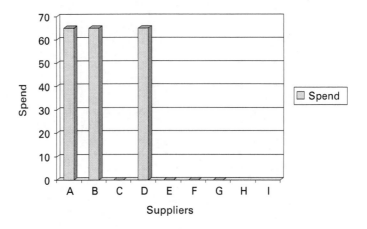

Figure 5.13   Spend mapping 4

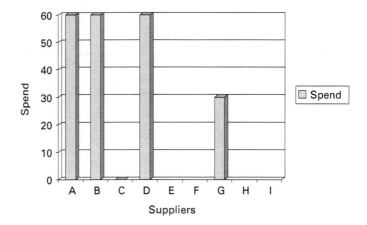

being supplier A. The buyer's first move was to get rid of suppliers E, F, G, H and I.

In the process, of course, he got bigger discounts from suppliers B, C and D and reduced the power of supplier A. This is shown in Figure 5.11.

He then got rid of supplier C, giving the business to suppliers A, B and D – at a bigger discount, of course (shown in Figure 5.12). He then brought back supplier G and threatened suppliers A, B and D that unless they gave him bigger discounts, most of his business would be given to supplier G!

It will by now be clear to readers that buyers like this have little understanding of the concept of value, even though, according to the Global

Value Proposition Vice President of SKF, companies that buy on total cost of ownership are 35 per cent more profitable than companies that do not.

Figure 5.14 Supplier relationships as a source of business advantage

	Type	Business contribution criteria	Business process criteria
10 10 <1% of suppliers	Strategic Suppliers	• 'First mover' advantage • Channels to market • Reverse revenue generation	• VP lead • Business strategy driven • 'A team' on both sides
20 600 C. 20% of all suppliers	Preferred Suppliers	• Point-to-point solution • Technology access • Operational advantage	• Relationship manager • Strategy from Catman • SLA scorecard
1,350 3,000 C. 80% of all suppliers	Commodity Suppliers	• Cost improvement • Superior service levels • Ease of transaction	• Managed locally • Performance monitored • E-enabled

Figure 5.15 'Must have' criteria drive hard and soft measures

1. Vision	• Sharing of long-term vision and orientation. • Global focus and commitment with service & support capability. • Defined but flexible boundaries.
2. Culture	• Similar or complementary values. • Understanding of the process to deal with differences. • Flexibility in approach since circumstances may change over time. • An exit route needs to exist.
3. Impact	• Maximum economic and strategic leverage, ie product/market differentiation. • Attainment of time to market, quality & productivity objectives. • Shareholder value creation. • Blending core competencies, leadership capabilities & complementary strengths (allowing outsourcing of non-core capability). • Adding real productivity & value (significant cost savings & revenue potential). • Globally focused, linkages to new business opportunities & capable of complementing the business focus. • Attainment of high performance, low cost & strategic objectives (producing unique design, integration & marketing capabilities).
4. Intimacy	• Readiness to share ideas & information. • Not overly locked into a competitor.
5. Balance	• An element of demonstrated commitment from both sides. • Readiness for risk-taking and sharing of costs. • Building trust and, thereby, moving to intimacy.

Figure 5.16   Strategic purchasing[4]

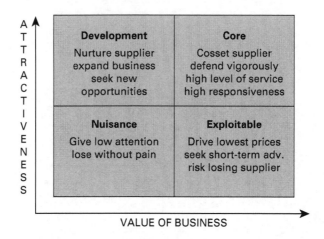

VALUE OF BUSINESS

The second type of professional buyer – the value seeker

Figures 5.14 and 5.15 are the criteria used by one multinational property company. Even a cursory glance at these will convince you that this company takes a highly professional approach to selecting its major suppliers and, unless they can meet these criteria, it will be almost impossible to be a meaningful supplier to this customer. Our experience from the Cranfield Best Practice Research Club over 20 years is that most major customers are developing sophisticated criteria like this.

At this point it is worth pointing out that most professional buying directors use a version of the matrix shown in Figure 5.16. It is a sad reflection on most companies that they reside in either the bottom left or the bottom right box and therefore trade mainly on price.

Those suppliers, however, who understand their customers' businesses well and the problems and issues they face and who develop financially quantified value propositions based on their customers' needs, are the ones who thrive and prosper and who create sustainable shareholder value added. In Chapter 6 we show how to analyse the needs of major customers.

Actions

1 Take a major customer and populate Figure 5.7 with the relevant information.

Figure 5.17   Which part of the market are we describing?

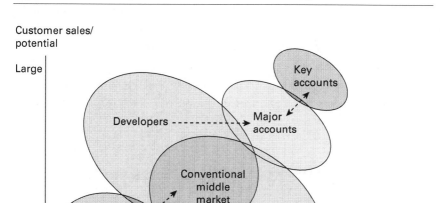

2 Draw boxes for each of your principal products or services together with who is responsible for selling them. Do the same for who is responsible for buying these in the customer's organization. Link them up according to how they relate to each other (refer to Figure 5.5).

   – Does your company offer the customers a key account manager as a single point of contact with appropriate authority?

   – Does the customer offer central purchasing through a single decision-making point?

   – Is your company organized to maximize its leverage with the customer?

2 How other customers buy

At this stage, it is important to spell out which part of the market we are describing, so we refer to Figure 5.17.

In section 1 of this chapter we described how major customers (top right of Figure 5.17) buy. Now we focus on the mass market shown in the middle of Figure 5.17. At this level, it is important to understand that value propositions need to be targeted at market segments (groups of customers with the same or similar needs).

There are two stages to this process. The first is understanding how the market works and the second is segmenting those who make the buying decisions.

Identifying the key decision-makers

In any market, 100 per cent of goods/services are 'made', distributed and bought, and it is essential to know what is happening in that particular market. We set out in some detail how market mapping should be carried out in order to identify decision-makers. The easiest junction to start the market map is the final user's junction, noting at each junction the volume/value (or percentage of the total market) decided there. It's always best to estimate these figures if they are not known.

Segmentation

If you have lost a bit of focus reading this chapter so far, don't despair, as in some cases market mapping isn't essential. It is, nonetheless, an extremely useful learning tool, so we advise you to have a go at producing one, using the template at the end of Chapter 4. **Market segmentation**, however, *is* essential, as it is the very cornerstone of successful business enterprise and we refer you to Chapter 2 for a method of completing this.

Actions

Describe how the key customers or segments in your market buy.

References

1 Wilson, C (1998) *Profitable Customers,* 2nd edition, Kogan Page, London.

2 Woodburn, D and McDonald, M (2013) *Key Account Management,* 3rd edition, John Wiley & Sons, Chichester.

3 Based on Woodburn, D and McDonald, M (2006) Unpublished Cranfield University research report.

4 Based on Kraljic, P (1983) Purchasing must become supply management, *Harvard Business Review*, September.

Which key accounts should you develop value propositions for?

06

Introduction

This chapter deals with key accounts only. Chapter 7 deals with which segments you should develop value propositions for.

Before we explore how to uncover the real needs of key accounts and market segments, we need to spell out a relatively simple process for categorizing them. This is worth devoting time to, otherwise an awful lot of energy will be wasted.

The whole point of this section is that no matter how hard you try, some customers will always be interested only in getting the lowest price. In these cases there is little point in expending energy on developing financially quantified value propositions only to have the usual debilitating argument about price, knowing that in the end they are going to choose the lowest price offer.

So, it will be a brilliant investment of your time to start the process by selecting those customers where your value proposition approach stands the best chance of success.

The point is that not all customers want or deserve value propositions.

We will start by looking more closely at key accounts.

Which key accounts are 'strategic'? How to select and define them

Key accounts are customers in a business-to-business market identified by selling companies as of strategic importance. Another way of looking at this is to say that a key account is a customer that should be treated as if it were a market in its own right. This doesn't mean all large customers, of course. A quick glance at Figure 6.1 indicates an approximate split between customers in a typical database.

From this it can be seen that in most cases the bulk of accounts will be either small or medium enterprises (SMEs), or larger mid-sized accounts, with only a few very large, powerful customers. The bulk of customers sit in the middle of Figure 6.1 and it is here that market segmentation must be carried out, as we spelled out in Chapter 2. The top right of the figure is where key accounts sit. But not all of them deserve the same level of attention when it comes to developing value propositions.

The first question most companies get the wrong answer to is, 'How many key accounts should we have?' One global telecommunications company claimed to have a thousand! But, as will be seen just from the amount of data alone that has to be collected in order to prepare a value proposition that aligns the supplier's resources with the customer's, it will never be possible to have more than, at most, 20 or thereabouts. At one stage, DHL

Figure 6.1   The customer portfolio

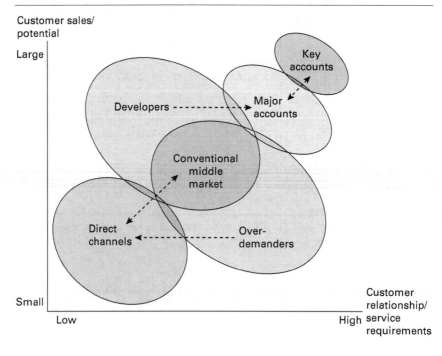

Worldwide had only 18 integrated key accounts globally, and each of these alone made more revenue and profit than any country profit centre.

In the case of companies, all of whom have limited resources for R&D, IT, HR, logistics, and so on, it would be impossible to commit them to more than a handful of projects in carefully selected key accounts. The proliferation of vast social media networks on Facebook and Twitter serve as stark examples that, while we can easily have hundreds of 'friends' and acquaintances, as individuals, we only devote a limited amount of genuine warmth and connection to a close-knit circle of friends and family.

The criteria for selecting which accounts should go into a company's key account programme are not set in concrete, but should obviously take account of the potential for growth in future time periods. So, in the main, they will be large and powerful. But frequently there are grounds for including smaller, more influential customers on the basis of the prestige that attaches itself to all their suppliers, or on the basis of future growth. For example, neither Virgin nor Microsoft would have been in many suppliers' key account programmes 30 years ago.

Figure 6.2 shows a well-accepted model for the initial categorization of key accounts. Figure 6.3 shows a real-world example from a global technology company.

So for now, let us aim for between 10 and 15 customers to be included in your key account value proposition programme.

Figure 6.2   Key account preliminary selection

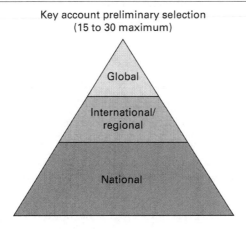

Figure 6.3   Customer segmentation in a major multinational

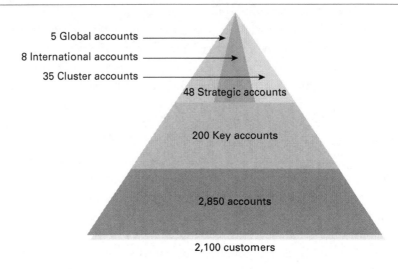

5 Global accounts

8 International accounts

35 Cluster accounts

48 Strategic accounts

200 Key accounts

2,850 accounts

2,100 customers

Let us also summarize so far:

- Do not include too many customers in your value proposition development programme.
- Do not put in only customers with whom you have a good relationship.
- Take account of potential growth in your selection.

Classifying key accounts: how to understand their differences

Once selected, it will be obvious when examining the list that they are all different in size, organizational structure, culture, requirements, behaviour, and so on. Also, your own relationships will range from non-existent to poor, to average, to very close, and these differences must be taken into account before even thinking about preparing strategic accounts for them. Figure 6.4 shows a well-accepted way of classifying key accounts based on our 20 years of research at Cranfield University School of Management's Global Best Practice Key Account Management Research Club.

To make Figure 6.4 more understandable, we have developed fictional representations of each KAM stage. These are shown in Figure 6.5, briefly describing each.

Figure 6.4   Different KAM relationship types[1]

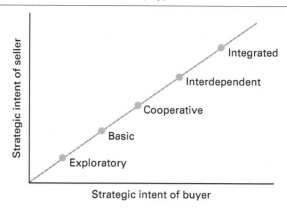

Each one of these relationship types is now described in more detail.

Figure 6.5 shows an exploratory, pre-trading phase, which is all about exploring the customer's needs.

The first, 'Exploratory', is all about pre-trading and exploring the customer's needs. The seller certainly needs to be patient at this stage. 'Basic KAM' looks like the well-known 'bow-tie' type of relationship. You have some business, but so do your competitors. It is a bit like the docking of a space station and a spacecraft – not very stable and if either the buyer or the key account manager leaves for any reason, the relationship might end.

The middle one, 'Cooperative KAM' is the most frequently encountered type of relationship that we have found in our 20 years of research at Cranfield University School of Management's KAM Best Practice Research Club. At this stage, you may be a preferred supplier, but only one of many and you will have multi-function contacts. The problem with this is that these multi-function contacts cost you a lot of money and you usually do not charge them. Consequentially, our research showed that this often leads to a loss-making situation for the supplier. Our advice is to move the relationship forwards or backwards, or at the very least to charge for all the services being provided. Otherwise the customer will take advantage of your generosity.

We will now spend a little more time on the last two types of relationship shown in Figure 6.5, 'Interdependent KAM' and 'Integrated KAM'.

As can be seen from the points below, a lot of careful exploratory work needs to take place before committing serious resources to this kind of potential key account.

Figure 6.5 Visualization of different KAM relationship types

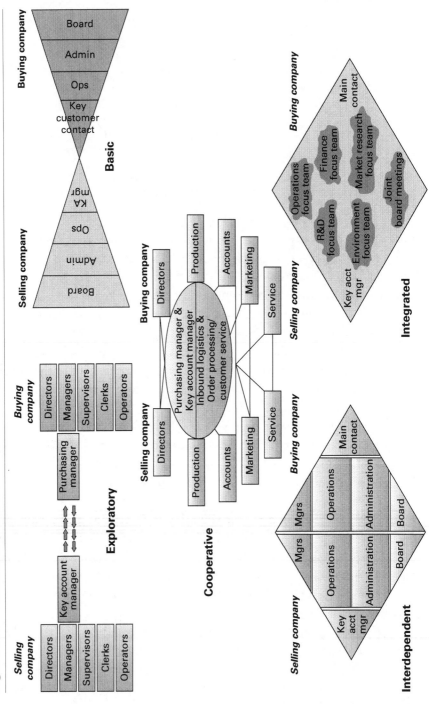

Figure 6.6   Interdependent Key Account Management[2]

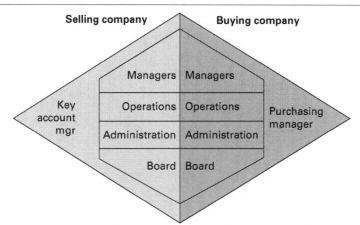

Interdependent KAM

Figure 6.6 illustrates the well-known 'diamond' relationships in key account management. In this type of relationship, interdepartmental relationships are properly organized by the buyer and the supplier's key account manager, although it will be observed that there is still a dividing line separating the two organizations.

The characteristics of interdependent relationships are shown below, from which it can be seen that, while both organizations are very close, the supplying company can still be dropped, albeit with some inconvenience, but not with really serious consequences:

- both acknowledge importance to each other;
- principal or sole supplier;
- exit more difficult;
- larger number of multi-functional contacts;
- developing social relationships;
- high volume of dialogue;
- streamlined processes;
- high level of information exchange, some sensitive;
- better understanding of customer;
- development of trust;

- proactive rather than reactive;
- prepared to invest in relationship;
- wider range of joint and innovative activity;
- joint strategic planning, focus on the future;
- opportunity to grow business.

Integrated KAM

Integrated KAM relationships, as illustrated in Figure 6.7, are the rarest of all relationships.

Open book accounting, for example, is a characteristic on the part of both supplier and customer and total trust is enjoyed between them. Often cost reductions are shared and added values are also shared, benefiting both parties equally. A mutual interdependence makes it virtually impossible for either party to drop the other, as both are as one, creating value in the marketplace.

Another characteristic is the existence of many interdisciplinary joint long-term projects. From this it will be obvious that only a handful of relationships can ever be like this because of limited specialist resources on both sides.

Figure 6.7   Integrated Key Account Management

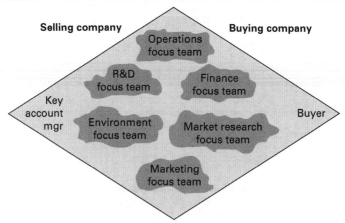

The characteristics of integrated relationships are summarized below:

- real partnership: complementary, mutually dependent;
- few in number;
- sole supplier, possible handling of secondary suppliers;
- high exit barriers, exit is traumatic;
- individual organizations subsidiary to team socially;
- dedicated, cross-boundary functional/project teams;
- open information-sharing on sensitive subjects;
- transparent costing systems;
- assumption of mutual trustworthiness, at all levels;
- abstention from opportunistic behaviour;
- lowered protection against opportunism;
- joint long-term strategic planning;
- better profits for both.

Mini case 1

Here we return to Porter's value chain.[3] The outline below shows Porter's value chain for a manufacturing organization. For 3M's integrated key accounts, at any point in time, they have several major joint projects with the customer's R&D, inbound logistics, operations, outbound logistics, sales and marketing, and after-sales service. The joint learning from such state-of-the-art companies keeps them continuously ahead of competitors and ensures long-term, stable and profitable relationships.

Support activities:

- infrastructure: legal, accounting, financial management;
- human resource management: personnel, pay, recruitment, training, manpower planning, etc;
- product and technology development: product and process design, production engineering, market testing, R&D, etc;
- procurement: supplier management, funding, subcontracting, specification.

Primary activities:

- inbound logistics: eg quality control, receiving raw material, control, etc;
- operations: eg manufacturing, packaging, production control, quality control, maintenance, etc;
- outbound logistics: eg finishing goods, order handling, despatch, delivery, invoicing, etc;
- sales and marketing: eg customer management, order taking, promotion, sales analysis, market research, etc;

Together:

$$\text{Value added} - \text{Cost} = \text{Profit}$$

Note: many activities cross the boundaries, especially information-based activities such as sales forecasting, capacity planning, resource scheduling, pricing, and so on.

Disintegrating KAM

Relationships can, of course, go sour. The list below shows the main causes. It is interesting to note that it is rarely for price reasons. Our research at Cranfield has shown that two of the most frequent reasons are a lack of skills on the part of the key account manager and breach of trust:

- occurs at any level;
- rarely caused by price problems;
- often change in key personnel;
- key account manager's approach or lack of skills;
- failure to forge multi-level links;
- breach of trust;
- prolonged poor performance against agreed programme;
- changing market positions;
- changing culture, organization, ownership, role;
- complacency;
- financial disappointment?

Companies who persist in promoting excellent sales people into key account roles without training them in the kind of general management skills required and who then compound their error by rewarding them purely on how much they sell are a constant source of irritation and annoyance to sophisticated customers who want to develop profitable relationships rather than be 'sold to' all the time. Breach of trust is another frequent cause of upset.

Mini case 2

The chairman of one major multinational supplier to the car and building industries blithely announced at the company's annual general meeting that their growth in profits had come largely from lower raw material costs. It doesn't take too much imagination to understand why, the following day, this company's phones were red hot with irate customers who hadn't been told about this and who felt they had been ripped off by this supplier!

Be realistic about key account relationships

For the rest of this chapter, we weave in a valuable methodology presented in Malcolm's 2017 publication with Beth Rogers, *Malcolm McDonald on Key Account Management.* Some sections are directly extracted and others adapted to suit this context. For more depth on this topic, you can purchase the full book here: https://bit.ly/2sS2WmC

From the above it can be deduced that the most profitable and desirable kind of relationship is the 'integrated' one. Alas, as stated above, such relationships are rare and, as can be seen, require substantial dedicated multi-functional resource requirements on the part of the supplier, although obviously the same applies on the customer side.

The main point, however, is that in selecting which customers and potential customers should be included in your programme for developing value propositions, there will inevitably be a mix of the different kinds of relationships described above and there may not be any interdependent or integrated accounts at all.

This doesn't matter as long as you are able to categorize all your key accounts in a logical and business-like way in order to manage each one appropriately for the purpose of generating the desired level of profitability, which will result in shareholder value added.

The next section of this chapter explains in detail how to do this. This is the most crucial chapter in the book, for the result of this process will determine everything that follows, including value proposition development for each key account, as well as plans and resourcing.

A very practical way to classify your key accounts

Please do not be put off by the fancy name that we will now use to show you how you can carry out this crucial stage of key account management. The authors call it 'KAM strategic planning matrix', but we promise you it is very practical, actionable and useful. From here on, we will refer to it as the SPM (the strategic planning matrix).

The KAM strategic planning matrix (SPM)

The purpose of the KAM strategic planning matrix (SPM) is to:

- Array all important key customers relative to each other in the context of:
  - the relative attractiveness of each for growing your future profitability;
  - The relative competitiveness of your company in each.
- Its purpose in the light of the conclusions from the above is to develop realistic value propositions to achieve your objectives.
- A by-product of this planning exercise is the ability to explain your firm's strategy clearly and unequivocally to relevant audiences.
- Please note: change the criteria, scores and weights to suit your company.

The process for completing the SPM follows.

Getting started (steps)

Step 1

The first step is to select the key accounts to be included in the SPM process. We suggest initially confining the list to 10 or fewer actual or potential key accounts. As we said above, please be open-minded about the accounts to be included. It doesn't matter at this stage if you don't actually trade with a particular customer. The point is that you believe it is important for your company that you do. This step is of crucial importance and you must think about the prospect of growing your profits over the next three years, not just next year.

Please use the template in Table 6.1. We refer to revenue as 'wallet size' in this figure.

Table 6.1 Template to calculate 'wallet-size' revenue

List target key customers here		
	Wallet size	**Our sales**
C1		
C2		
C3		
C4		
C5		
C6		
C7		
C8		
C9		
C10		
Enter approximate wallet size and your sales in each		

Table 6.2 Key customer attractiveness factors

C attractiveness factors	10–7	6–4	3–0	X weight
Revenue				15
Growth potential%				30
Profit potential%				40
'Soft' factors				15
				100

So you have now selected your 10 key accounts.

Step 2

Now you have to list your 10 key accounts on a kind of thermometer, with 'high' at the top and 'low' at the bottom. 'High' will mean those accounts that offer the best prospect for any relevant competitor (not just you) to grow their profit over the next three years, so we will label this vertical axis: 'account attractiveness'. In order to do this dispassionately, you will need a logical set of criteria. We suggest the criteria shown in Table 6.2. This is only an example.

You and your directors must decide what an attractive potential revenue is for your company. For example, is it more than £10 million a year, or is it more than £0.5 million a year? You must then decide what a 'medium' and 'low' potential revenue is.

Then you must decide what is an attractive margin (return on sales – ROS) that any competitor could make out of a customer.

Next, you must decide what an attraction growth rate is.

The reason we have chosen these three attractiveness factors is because it is revenue, multiplied by ROS, multiplied by % growth, that equals profit, which is what we are interested in.

We have added a fourth attractiveness factor – 'soft factors' – solely as an example, in case you want to add more attractiveness factors, but we suggest you stick to just the three – revenue, % ROS and % growth over the three-year planning cycle.

Step 3

Referring again to Figure 6.2, you now have to decide which of the three or four account attractiveness factors you chose is less or more important (we refer to this as 'weighting factors'). For example, if you have a factory and have only 40 per cent capacity, you might decide to give 'revenue' and '% growth' a higher weight than % ROS. On the other hand, if you are working at full capacity, you may decide to give '% ROS' a higher weight than 'revenue' and '% growth'.

You need to think very carefully about all of this because when you score out of 10 each account against the above criteria and multiply the score by the weight, this will determine its position on the 'thermometer' – the vertical axis.

You will soon appreciate how important this point of the exercise is, as it is a crucial determinant of how you set objectives and strategies and allocate your scarce resources.

Please use Table 6.2 for this purpose.

Step 4

Score each key customer according to the parameters you have used in Table 6.2. Then multiply the score by the weight (also in Table 6.2).

Place each key customer on the 'thermometer' – the vertical axis, from low to high. Ensure that the scale reflects the spread of scores. For example, if the lowest score is 3.5, make the vertical axis start at 3.0. If the highest score is 6.5, make 8.0 the highest point on the scale. This will ensure that each of your 10 accounts is spread out on the scale.

It is also important to remember that an account lower down the vertical axis is not 'unattractive'. It merely means that it is less attractive than one higher up the vertical axis in its ability to grow your profits over the next three years.

Step 5

Evaluate your strengths in each key account relative to your most relevant competitor. Do this initially intuitively for the purpose of this exercise. Then do it properly when you have more time. We will show you how to do this in Chapter 7.

Table 6.3 is an example of a more quantitative way of doing this. Please note that this will take time, because each of your key accounts will have

Table 6.3 Quantitative method

KEY CUSTOMER NAME	CSFs	WEIGHT	Score x Weight	You	Comp 1	Comp 2
	eg. Reputation	50				
	eg. Cost	10				
	eg. After-sales services	15				
	eg. Resources/compatibility	25				
		100				

Weighted
Score X/1000

Use these weighted scores to quantify each on the horizontal axis (again, ensure your highest weighted scores and lowest weighted scores reflect your range of scores. DO NOT USE A SCALE OF 10 _____ 0 on the horizontal axis! Even if all the KAM scores are relatively similar, you will still have greater or lesser strengths in each, so put the highest scores on the left and the lower scores on the right. However, if time-constrained, place each account on the horizontal axis using your qualitative judgement.

different critical success factors (CSF) and you will have to complete your assessment for every one of your key accounts.

Step 6

Now find the points of intersection for each of your 10 key accounts on a four-box matrix. See Figure 6.8.

Step 7

Draw circles for each key account market, the volume of each representing its wallet size.

Step 8

Draw circles for your sales in each key account, one inside the other.

Step 9

Draw conclusions for your organization.

Step 10

Taking the circles with your sales only, in each key account, set revenue objectives for each three years from now:

Figure 6.8   Four-box matrix (the SPM) – points of intersection

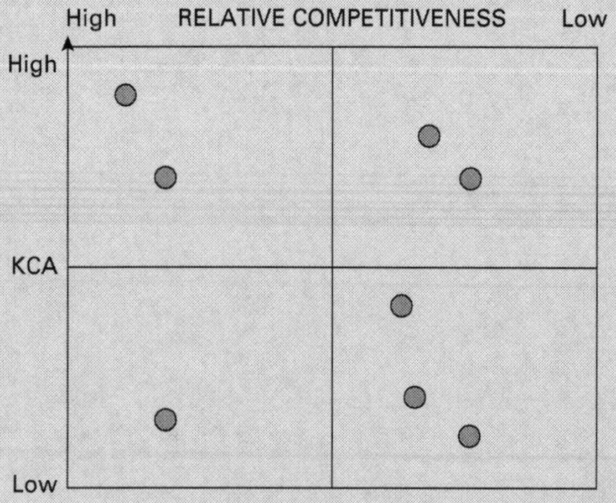

- The circles will grow, decline, or stay the same.
- They can only move to the left or right or stay where they are.
- They *cannot* move vertically, as 'attractiveness' means future attractiveness over the next three to five years.

Before setting revenue objectives, see our guidelines for each of the four boxes (given in Table 6.4).

Please note that we refer to KAs in the top left box of Figure 6.10 as 'strategic customers'. KAs in the bottom left box we call 'status customers'. KAs in the top right box we call 'star customers'. Finally, KAs in the bottom right box we call 'streamline customers'.

These labels reflect the reality of their importance to the supplier. A completed example is given in Figure 6.9.

Important conclusions/actions

We fully understand the crucial importance of setting objectives and strategies for key accounts, and these will be dependent on the position of each in the SPM. We will, therefore, return to these two key steps later in this book.

Table 6.4 Objectives and strategies suggested by the key customer strategic planning matrix

Category	Description
Strategic customers	• Very important customers, but the relationship has developed still further, to the level of partnership. The relationship is 'win-win'; both sides have recognised the benefits they gain from working together. Customers buy not on price but on the added value derived from being in partnership with the supplier. The range of contacts is very broad and joint plans for the future are in place. Products and services are developed side-by-side with the customer. Because of their large size and the level of resource which they absorb, only a few customers fall into this category.

(*continued*)

Table 6.4 (*Continued*)

Category	Description
Status customers	• Very important customers (in terms of value). Commit to security of supply and offer products and services which are tailored to the customer's particular needs. Price is less important in the customer's choice of supplier. Both parties have some goals in common. The two organizations have made some form of commitment to each other. Invest as necessary in these customers in order to continue the business relationship for mutual advantage, but do not over invest.
Star customers	• Price is still a major factor in the decision to buy but security of supply is very important and so is service. Spend more time with some of these customers and aim to develop a deeper relationship with them in time.
Streamline customers	• These customers usually want a standard product, 'off the shelf'. Price is the key factor in their decision to buy. Do not invest large amount of time in the business relationship at this stage.

Figure 6.9 Portfolio analysis – strategic planning matrix (SPM)

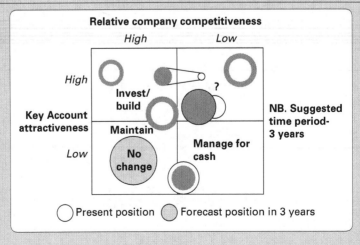

For now, even if you aren't keen to follow the process we have set out in the chapter, we would like you to have a go at producing an SPM to appreciate that not all key accounts are created equal and that your value propositions for each should reflect your wish to grow your profits over the next three years from a portfolio of accounts. The following two simple examples should be sufficient to explain what we mean.

Case history 1

If you look at the big circle at the bottom of Figure 6.10, this was a massive, global publishing company that had decided to rationalize its paper suppliers, choosing only two who would give them the lowest price. One of their current suppliers was a big player in the market, and because they had high fixed costs with their paper mills, they could not afford to lose the substantial volume of paper production, should they lose this account, as their fixed costs would remain and have to be spread over a much reduced volume of paper production.

We advised them to enter the bidding process in order to win the contract, even at a ridiculously low price. Furthermore, when they had won their unattractive contract, we advised the supplier merely to meet the terms of the contract and to charge extra for anything outside the contract, as well as minimizing the costs to serve this customer.

The point of the story is that it may well be that there is a big, important customer which does not offer much potential for growth in profits – hence their position in the bottom right box of the SPM. The other point is that the advice given in Table 6.4 surely now begins to make sense.

Figure 6.10   Categorizing key clients by potential for growth in the firm's profits[4]

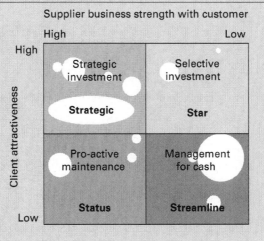

Case history 2

Figure 6.11 shows a real SPM for a company serving clients in the financial services market.

It will be seen that the biggest and most attractive client was the Thompson Group, with an annual spend of £32 million – a spend that was growing year by year. The problem for this particular supplier was that they were rated by the customer as the worst of all suppliers – hence the client's position in the top right box of the SPM. The reason for this was that the accounting bias of the supplier was encouraging managers of this account to manage it for profit maximization, whereas even a modicum of common sense would have informed them that they should have been investing in this client in order to move it across to the top left box.

It was only by positioning the Thompson Group in the context of all the other clients in an SPM that the senior managers became aware of the profit-maximizing mentality of the supplier, which was over time leading to the very opposite result.

Figure 6.11 Key client selection matrix tool

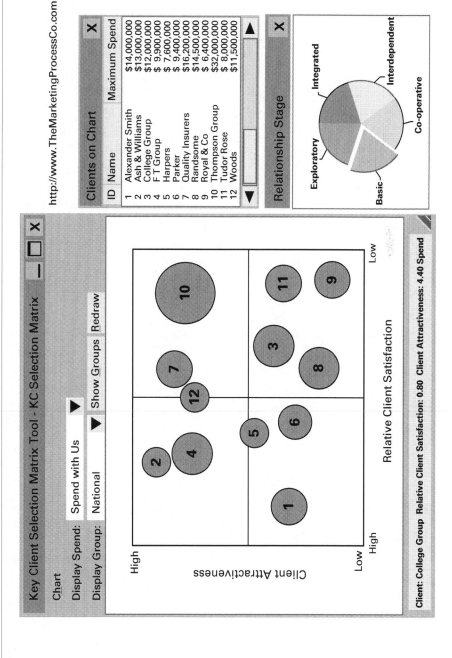

The relevance of this to the development of value propositions

We refer you again to Figure 6.4, the SPM guidelines, and to Figure 6.10.

The point about status customers (bottom left) is that there is not much potential for growing your profits over the next three years and you already have a relative competitive advantage over your competitors. In these cases, you must beware of complacency, so you will need to keep a close eye on developments and threats to them and you will need to ensure that any value propositions you develop help to keep your competitive advantage.

Customers in the top left box (strategic customers) represent most of your future growth, so you should continuously work hard at developing and updating your value propositions. This is undoubtedly your priority.

Customers in the top right box (star customers) represent a challenge to you, as they are very attractive, given their potential for growing your profits. The problem is that they prefer other suppliers, so your relative competitive position is weak. Of course, you should develop value propositions for all of these customers, but as this requires a lot of hard work and resources, as you will see in Chapters 8 and 9, you need to prioritize one or two of them to concentrate on.

These will probably be the ones like the Thompson Group in Figure 6.11. In cases like this, it is important not to worry too much about the time, effort and resources dedicated to developing value propositions. In other words, do not let your accountants use the age-old argument about current profitability. Here, you are developing value propositions to build better relationships, which will lead to future profitability.

That leaves one box, of course – the bottom right (streamline customers). Here, not only are you competitively relatively weak, but there is not much opportunity for growing your profits. Here, develop value propositions only when you can see an opportunity for growing your profits.

Far be it from us to suggest that you shouldn't develop value propositions for all customers. It is just that this takes time and resources, so we suggest you use the analysis recommended in this chapter to prioritize your time and effort.

In Chapter 7, we show how the same principles should be applied to market segments.

Actions

Try your hand at determining what criteria you would use for the vertical axis of the SPM and the relative importance of each (a weight out of 100).

For your 10 selected accounts, use your criteria to score and weight each one so that you have them spread out on a kind of thermometer, with the most attractive ones at the top and the less attractive ones near the bottom.

Then do a very rough approximation of your relative strengths versus competitors and produce a first-cut SPM. We will show you how to calculate the horizontal axis in Chapter 8.

References

1 Millman, A and Wilson, K (1995) From key account selling to key account management, *Journal of Marketing Practice*, **1** (1), pp 9–22.

2 Based on Woodburn, D and McDonald, M (2006) Unpublished Cranfield University research report.

3 Porter, M (1980) *Competitive Strategy*, Free Press, New York.

4 Adapted from Woodburn, D and McDonald, M (2013) *Key Account Management*, 3rd edition, John Wiley & Sons, Chichester.

Which segments 07 should you develop value propositions for?

Introduction

This is a shorter chapter because the methodology for the strategic planning matrix (SPM) is exactly the same as in Chapter 6. The only difference is that instead of 'key accounts', read 'segments' or groups of customers. We will, however, start by repeating an earlier figure as Figure 7.1.

We are now going to concentrate on the mass market in the middle of Figure 7.1 and assume you have read and acted on Chapter 2 on market segmentation. The first issue, then, is to find a way of filtering the hundreds of accounts in the middle of Figure 7.1. We are pleased to set out a new-to-the-world (but tried and tested) process for doing this.

Targeting mid-sized B2B customers by their potential to succeed

This 'potential to succeed' is based on a marketing strategy competence test that research at Cranfield University School of Management carried out by Dr Brian Smith and supervised by Professor Malcolm McDonald has shown to be a good proxy for identifying companies with a good future.

This particular version of the questionnaire is for a company to complete about its business customers.

For those B2B customers identified as being important to the business, they can then be analysed in terms of the different needs they are looking to have met by their supplier so that the correct propositions can be put together for them. This second-stage analysis would follow the McDonald/ Dunbar market segmentation process (not covered in this book).[1]

Figure 7.1   The customer portfolio

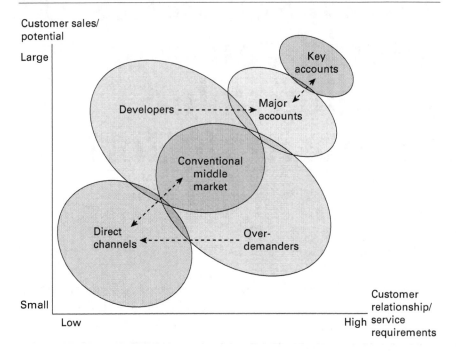

Which of the following best describes how this customer operates in its own market?

1   Concentration of sales and marketing efforts

   1.1   They target all customers in the market – score 0

   1.2   They focus on particular customer groups differentiated by who they are (ie by business sector, by their size) or by their location – score 1

   1.3   They focus on particular customer groups differentiated by the needs they have – score 2

   1.4   Unknown/it's not clear – score 0

2   Extent to which their marketing strategy directs which sales and marketing actions they should follow and which they should avoid

   2.1   They have complete freedom of action (within the confines of their capabilities) – score 0

2.2 Their marketing strategy imposes some constraints but there is still a high level of freedom – score 1

2.3 Their marketing strategy is very specific about most of what they should do – score 3

2.4 Unknown/it's not clear – score 0

3　Understanding of competitive advantage

3.1 They aren't clear and can't substantiate why customers should choose them rather than their competitors – score 0

3.2 They put forward reasons why customers should choose them but can't substantiate them – score 1

3.3 They clearly understand why customers should choose them and have market-based proof to back it up – score 2

3.4 Unknown/it's not clear – score 0

4　Use of its relevant internal strengths which contribute to its marketing strategy

4.1 They don't attempt to use the relevant strength(s) of any department in their marketing strategy – score 0

4.2 They use the relevant strengths of one or two departments and ignore the relevant strengths of others – score 1

4.3 They capitalize on the relevant strengths of all departments in their marketing strategy – score 2

4.4 Unknown/it's not clear – score 0

5　Differentiation from its competitors

5.1 They are a clone of their competitors and present a similar offer to the same customers (with any differentiation being of little significance) – score 0

5.2 They target different customers with similar offers to their competitors – score 1

5.3 They target the same or different customers with different offers – score 2

5.4 Unknown/it's not clear – score 0

6　Extent to which they meet customer needs

6.1 Their offers meet only the basic functional needs associated with the core product/service – score 0

6.2 Their offers not only meet the basic functional needs but also the needs associated with supporting services (before- and after-sales services, distribution, guarantees, add-ons, etc) – score 1

6.3 Their offers meet basic and supporting service needs plus the intangible needs of their customers (brand name, reputation, image, etc) – score 2

6.4 Unknown/it's not clear – score 0

7 Extent to which they take into account competitors' strategies

7.1 They appear oblivious to what their competitors are doing – score 0

7.2 They take into account some, but not all of their competitors' strategies – score 1

7.3 They take full cognizance of their competitors' strategies in what they do – score 2

7.4 Unknown / it's not clear – score 0

8 Extent to which they take into account forecast changes in uncontrollable external factors (technological, legislative, social, etc) which may impact them

8.1 They only go as far as today and tackle tomorrow when it comes – score 0

8.2 They take into account some, but not all of the forecast changes – score 1

8.3 They take account all of the forecast changes – score 2

8.4 Unknown/it's not clear – score 0

9 Countering their relative weaknesses compared with the competition which affect their ability to succeed in their market

9.1 They neither address their weaknesses nor try to diminish them by boosting their strengths – score 0

9.2 They are trying to fix their weaknesses either directly or by boosting their strengths – score 1

9.3 The strength of their strategy makes their weaknesses irrelevant – score 2

9.4 Unknown/it's not clear – score 0

10 Use of its relative strengths compared with the competition which affect their ability to succeed in their market

 10.1 They make little or very limited use of their strengths – score 0

 10.2 They are trying to make use of their strengths – score 1

 10.3 Their strategy highlights their strengths and builds them up – score 2

 10.4 Unknown/it's not clear – score 0

11 Ability to achieve its financial and non-financial objectives

 11.1 Their strategy will not deliver the objectives – score 0

 11.2 Their strategy will only deliver the financial objectives – score 1

 11.3 Their strategy will deliver all the objectives – score 2

 11.4 Unknown/it's not clear – score 0

12 Adequacy of resources (physical resources, financial resources and staff capabilities) to implement their strategy successfully

 12.1 They don't have the resources to implement their strategy – score 0

 12.2 They have one but not the other type of resource – score 1

 12.3 They are fully resourced to implement their strategy – score 2

 12.4 Unknown/it's not clear – score 0

How did this customer score?

As a guideline: 18–24 – going places and pretty well guaranteed to succeed.

  12–17 – they will succeed, as long as the competition is weak.

  6–11 – they will survive as long as the competition is weak.

  > 6 – not much hope for the future.

Plotting the results

Now use Figure 7.2 on the following page to plot these scores.

Take the top and bottom scores and set the highest score on the vertical axis to the top score plus one and set the lowest score on the vertical axis to the bottom score less one. Spread the scores evenly along the axis and position each customer on the vertical axis according to their score.

Figure 7.2   Current spend in market versus market capability

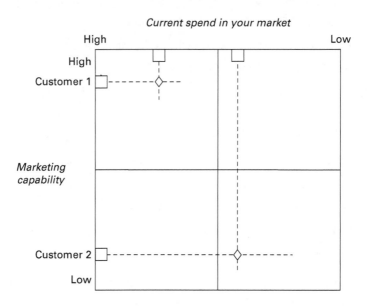

Using the range of current spend in your market of these customers, set the high position on the horizontal axis to the highest spend rounded up to the next whole unit of measure (so if spend is in millions, it's the next million) and set the low position on the horizontal axis to the lowest spend rounded down to the next whole unit of measure. Spread the spend evenly along the axes and for each customer on the vertical axis locate their position on the horizontal axis and mark the point of intersection.

Determine your cut-off points for marketing capability and current spend in order to isolate the customers you need to focus on. These are the customers for whom there is a future and with whom you need to develop your business.

Now flag any customers outside these boundaries who are currently important to you (which will usually be because of their current spend in your market). These are customers of the present, and for those of them with poor marketing capability scores, their revenue is revenue you will need to replace in the future. For those customers outside your boundaries but with acceptable marketing capability scores, you may need to develop your business with them in order to achieve your financial objectives, if these objectives cannot be achieved by the customers originally isolated by your cut-off points.

To develop your business with the customers isolated by the above process, it is important to understand how to win their orders and beat the competition. You can be sure, however, that these customers do not have the same requirements and will require different value propositions. The next stage, therefore, is to split these customers into different groups, or segments, within which customers share the same level of interest in the same, or comparable, set of needs satisfied by a distinct marketing proposition.

This is where the market segmentation process set out in Chapter 2 should be used.

But even if you don't want to go down this segmentation route, by using this methodology you will still end up with a group of customers in the top left box for whom developing value propositions is likely to produce excellent results.

This is where you should be focusing your value proposition development process.

Further refinement and focus

It is now possible to use the same methodology spelled out in Chapter 6 to refine your target customers even more tightly. This is called the strategic planning matrix (SPM). All you need to do is change the word 'account' for 'segment' or 'customer'.

We are now ready to move on to how to understand customer needs.

Actions

Complete the targeting exercise spelled out in this chapter.

Reference

1 McDonald, M and Dunbar, I (2012) *Market Segmentation,* 4th edition, John Wiley & Sons, Chichester.

Understanding key account and segment needs before building a value proposition

08

Introduction

This chapter is perhaps the most important in the book. It is where the hard work really begins. But don't despair, as the payoff will make it all worthwhile.

We saw the basis on which key accounts should be defined and selected in Chapter 6. This can be summarized diagrammatically in Figure 8.1. The purpose of this chapter is to provide a set of specific and detailed procedures for key account analysis prior to developing value propositions for each key account selected as being worthy of focused attention.

An overview of the total process, which we have called the business partnership process, is given in Figure 8.2.

Steps 1–5 might cause you to question whether devoting time to this kind of analysis is worth your while. Our experience, however, is that world-class organizations do this kind of analysis on all their targeted customers because the more they understand about their customers' business, the more likely they are to have a deep understanding of the issues they face. Even more importantly, they can tailor their value propositions to all those who influence which goods and services they will buy and from whom. Having said all of this, the major benefits emerge from steps 6 and 7.

Steps 1 to 2 should ideally be carried out by 'headquarters' personnel. How to do this was spelled out in Chapters 2 and 3, so it is not necessary to repeat them here.

Figure 8.1   Key account strategies: a four-box strategic planning matrix

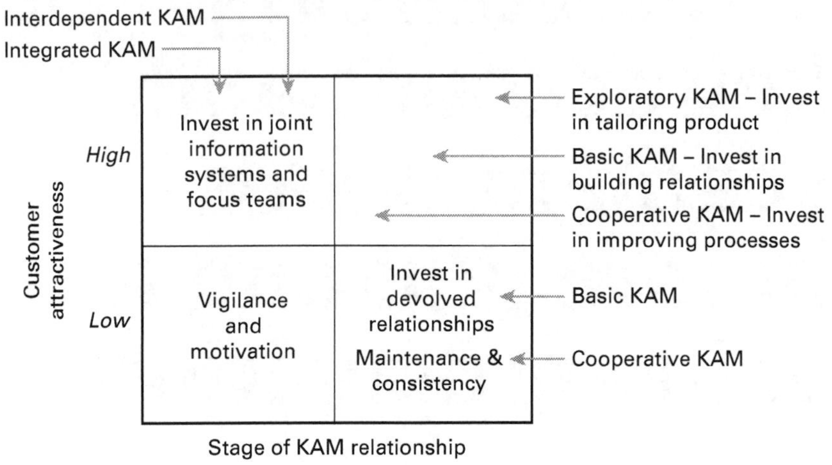

This chapter is devoted to describing each of the remaining steps involved in key account analysis, beginning with step 3 from Figure 8.2.

Key account analysis

Before it is possible to develop value propositions for key accounts, a detailed analysis of each key account must be undertaken by each individual key account manager and their team, somewhat in the manner of conducting a marketing audit. This is step 3 in Figure 8.2.

Step 3: industry driving forces analysis

Figure 8.3 shows an overall picture of the kind of analysis that needs to be carried out in order to understand key accounts better, *in particular the environment in which they are operating today.*

Figure 8.4 shows some of the detail that needs to be understood about the political/legal, economic, social, ecological and technical environment in which key accounts operate. A template to summarize these external influences is shown in Figure 8.5.

Figure 8.2 Business partnership process

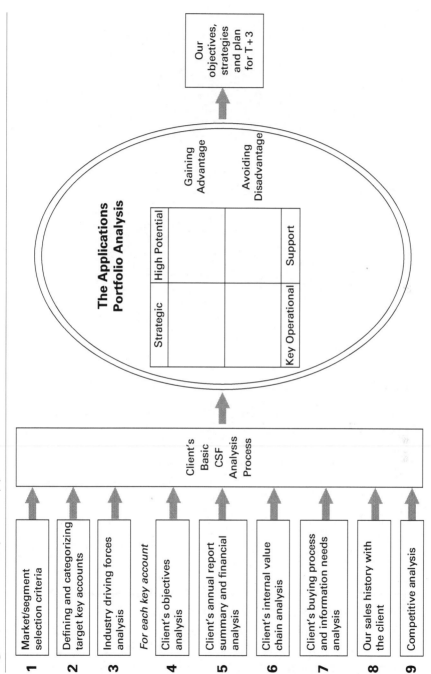

Figure 8.3   Macro environment

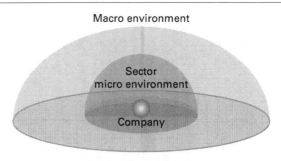

Figure 8.4   Macro environment influences: Steep

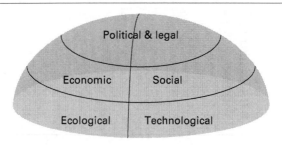

Table 8.1   Worksheet: STEEP analysis of customer's environment

STEEP factor	Challenges for customer	Importance S/M/L	In what ways can we help?
Social			
Technological			
Economic			
Ecological			
Political/legal			

Figure 8.5 shows the micro environmental influences affecting key accounts. These will now be expanded on.

The main point of step 3 is known as Porter's industry five forces analysis. It is taken from Porter's book *Competitive Strategy*[1] and has been of enormous value to generations of managers since its appearance in 1980.

Put simply, any industry has a number of competitors and the relative performance of these competitors is determined by recognizable forces:

Figure 8.5   Micro environment influences

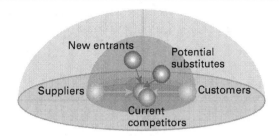

- potential entrants: the threat of new entrants and barriers to entry; economies of scale; product differentiation; capital requirements; switching costs; access to distribution channels; cost disadvantages additional to scale; government policy; entry deterring price; experience;

- customers: powerful if they make up a large proportion of the seller's sales; they make up a high proportion of buyer's costs; undifferentiated products; low buyer switching costs; threat of backward integration; the seller's product is not important to quality of buyer's product;

- potential substitute products and services creating threat;

- the power of suppliers: powerful if there are few suppliers; no substitutes; industry not important; customer of supplier group; supplier group's products are differentiated; threat to forward integration.

The words aptly describe the implications of each of the four outside forces on the competitors and it is clear that all competitors in a sector or industry will be affected by these driving forces.

This analysis is obviously best done by someone in central support services, perhaps marketing, as there is little point in a number of key account managers in the same industry all spending their time conducting the same analysis. If this is not practicable, the job will indeed have to be done be individual key account managers for their own sectors.

It must be stressed, however, that such an analysis is a prerequisite to the individual account analysis described later, as it provides key account managers with a deep analysis of their customers' industry and how it works and affects their performance.

Table 8.2 is a template to summarize in a relevant way the outcome of Porter's five forces analysis in terms of the opportunities and threats that face the customer.

Table 8.2   Worksheet: customer's Porter analysis

Market participants	Challenges for customer	Importance H/M/L	In what ways can we help?
Customer's customers			
Customer's competitors (current, new, potential)			
Suppliers to customers			

It should also be stressed here that steps 4–9 are all concerned with the analysis/diagnosis stage, which should be completed for each account before developing value propositions for them.

Step 4: customer's objectives analysis

The template given in Table 8.2 should be completed for each key account being targeted. It can be seen that the intention is to take the industry driving forces analysis and apply it specifically to an individual account in order to understand better what advantages and disadvantages it has. The main reason for doing this is to help you to understand ways in which your products or services may enable the client to exploit advantages and minimize disadvantages.

Each heading is intended merely to act as a trigger for some powerful conclusions about your client's competitive situation. This information will be used along with the further information to be gathered in steps 5–9.

Step 5: customer's annual report summary and financial analysis

Figure 8.6 enables a summary to be made of a careful reading and analysis of a customer's published annual report. Even if there is not a formal report published for the shareholders (say, for example, if your client is a subsidiary or division of a larger company), the directors do nonetheless tend to produce internal reports and newsletters which can be used instead.

Such documents can be a major source of information on what your customer believes to be the major issues facing them, their achievements and their objectives and strategies – in other words, their hopes for the future.

Figure 8.6 Annual report summary

1 MAJOR ACHIEVEMENTS	
2 MAJOR PROBLEMS/ISSUES	
3 OBJECTIVES	
4 STRATEGIES	
5 IN WHAT WAYS CAN WE HELP?	

It is always possible to extract valuable information which can be used in helping you understand how your organization might be of assistance. This information can now be put alongside the information gleaned from the previous objectives analysis summary.

Figure 8.7 focuses on the financial affairs of your customer and concerns information which can also be obtained from annual reports and other published sources. At first sight, this might appear to be some way removed from the reality of selling goods and services to a major account. However, a little thought will reveal that most organizations today are acutely aware of their financial performance indicators:

- current ratios;
- net profit margins;
- return on assets;
- debtor control;
- asset turnover.

The purpose of the analysis contained in Figure 8.7 is to make you acutely aware of the financial issues faced by your customer and to encourage you to explore whether any of your products and services could improve any of these ratios.

It will be obvious that any supplier who has taken the trouble to work out what impact its products and services have on the customer's bottom line will be preferred to a potential supplier who focuses only on product features.

Figure 8.7   Financial analysis – cash flow and balance sheet impact statement

Financial ratio indicator	Formula	Source					Company standing	Industry standing	Does it appear as though improvement is needed?		
		Annual report							Yes	No	
Current ratio	Current assets Current liabilities										
Net profit margin	Net profit Net sales										
Return on assets	Net profit Total assets										
Collection period	Debtors less bad debt Average day's sales										
Stock turnover	Cost of goods sold Stock										

Step 6: customer internal value chain analysis

This is the principal piece of analysis that needs to be carried out.

The concept of an organization's internal value chain was popularized by Professor Michael Porter in his book on competitive strategies, which was referred to earlier. It is assumed that readers are familiar with this concept. The value chain is introduced here as an invaluable tool in understanding how a major account actually functions. The bottom level shows bought-in goods or services entering the organization, passing through operations and then moving out to their markets through distribution, marketing and sales and service, for example:

- inbound logistics: receiving and warehousing materials, inventory control, transportation, scheduling to manufacture, quality control;
- operation: manufacturing, packaging, production control, quality control, repairs and maintenance;

- outbound logistics: finished goods, order handling, dispatch, delivery, invoicing;

- sales and marketing: customer management, order taking, promotion, sales analysis, market research;

- servicing: warranty, maintenance, education and training, upgrades.

Sitting above these core processes are organizational support activities such as:

- administrative: accounting, financial management, legal;

- human resource management: recruitment, training, succession planning, performance management, etc;

- product and technology development: product and process design, production engineering, market testing, R&D;

- procurement: supplier management, funding, subcontracting, specification.

Together the primary and support activities:

$$\text{Profit} = \text{Sales minus Costs}$$

Investigating how a major account actually manages these core activities can be a substantial task for a key account team, involving, as it does, an in-depth understanding of the detailed processes of the customer. This could include, for example, understanding what happens to your goods when they are delivered, where they are stored, how they are handled, how they are moved, how they are unpacked, how they are used and so forth. The purpose of such detailed analysis is to explore what issues and problems are faced by your customer with a view to resolving them through improvements and innovations.

The following is a very simple illustration of some of these issues and how they could be improved, thus representing sources of differentiation in the value chain. For readers operating in a service environment, Figure 8.8 gives an example of how Porter's value chain can be adapted – in this case for the financial services industry.

All information emanating from this analysis can be usefully summarized using a format similar to that shown in Table 8.3. There are four general headings of customer benefits:

1 possibilities for increased revenue for the customer;

2 possibilities for cost displacement;

3 possibilities for cost avoidance;

4 intangible benefits.

Another way of looking at this is to identify the methods of gaining competitive edge through value in use.

At this stage, Figure 8.3 should just be used for the purposes of making preliminary notes, as a financially quantified version of this will be given in Chapter 10.

Sources of differentiation in the value chain include:

- inbound logistics: handling this minimizes damage;

- operations: unique product features; conforms to specs; low defect rate; responsiveness to design change;

- outbound logistics: rapid and timely delivery; accurate order processing; careful handling to reduce damage;

- marketing and sales: high sales force coverage; superior technical literature; best credit terms; personal relations with buyers;

- service: rapid installation; high service quality; wide service coverage.

For service companies such as independent financial advisors (IFAs), this version may be more appropriate. For each key account, list ways in which you can use your resources/skills (eg e-commerce) to improve their value chain, by reducing their costs, by avoiding costs, or by creating value for their customers.

Figure 8.8 Internal value chain: service companies, eg IFAs

						Reducing cost	Creating value
Infrastructure	– Legal, accounting, financial management						
Human resource management	– Personnel, pay, recruitment, training, manpower planning, etc						
Product & technology development	– Product and process design, market testing, R&D, etc						
Procurement	– Supplier management, funding, subcontracting, specification						

Recognize exchange potential	Initiate dialogue	Exchange information	Negotiate/ tailor	Commit	Exchange value	Monitor	
							Reducing cost
							Creating value

Table 8.3 Worksheet: customer's value chain-based opportunities, including finance

Value chain	Describe opportunity for customer	Importance to customer H/M/L	Supplier's solution
Inbound			
Operations			
Outbound			
Marketing & sales			
Customer service			
Finance			
Procurement			
Technology development			
HR management			
Firm infrastructure			

Mini case 1: value chain analysis for a packaging company

An international chemical company undertook this investigation process using a novel method. They organized a two-day event for eight very senior people from different functions in a large packaging company. These executives included marketing people, a health and safety executive, an environmental specialist, a logistics manager, a manufacturing manager and a couple of directors! These executives were matched by equivalent managers and directors from the supplying company. An independent consultant was asked to chair the two-day event.

The purpose of the event, which was held in a neutral location, was to investigate ways in which the several goods and services of the supplying company were received, used and perceived by the customer. This inquiry was obviously only possible because of the good relationships already enjoyed by the supplier.

While it took a few hours for the independent moderator to break down the natural barriers to honest and open communication, the event had a major impact on the processes and attitudes of the supplier. For example, at one stage the customers were asked to go into a syndicate room and write down all the things they did not like or found inadequate in the supplying company. The sheer size of the list and the contents so shocked the supplier that it immediately agreed to set up a number of functional and cross-functional working groups comprising executives from both sides in order to study how cost-effective improvements could be made.

All issues were investigated openly and honestly, ranging from the strategic issues faced by the customer in its industry, to very tactical issues concerned with processes. The end result was a dramatically improved relationship which led to substantial benefits to both sides.

It is not suggested that this is the only way to discover the kind of detailed information outlined in Table 8.3. In many cases, much patience is required over considerable periods of time and the effectiveness and efficiency with which this investigative task can be carried out will be a function of how good and deep the existing relationships are.

Nonetheless it is difficult to see how improvements can be made without a thorough understanding of the customer's systems and processes.

The list of possibilities for improvement for the supplier (hence value propositions) is now growing quite considerably. However, there are still more aspects of the business which need to be analysed.

Step 7: the customer's buying process

You have already seen Figure 8.9 in Chapter 8. We expand further here about the buying process for both goods and services – a crucial stage in understanding the needs of key accounts. The same process applies equally well to both products and services.

Selling to an organization can be a complex process because it is possible for a number of different people to become involved at the customer end. Although theoretically only one of these is the buyer, in practice he or she might not be allowed to make a decision to purchase until others with technical expertise or hierarchical responsibility have given their approval.

The personal authority of the buyer will to a large extent be governed by the following factors:

1 *The cost of the product* – the higher the cost, the higher up in the organization the purchasing decision will be made.

2 *The 'newness' of the product* – the relative novelty of the product will pose an element of commercial risk for an organization. A new and untried proposition will require support at a senior management level, whereas a routine, non-risky product can be handled at a lower level.

Figure 8.9 Buying process for goods and services

Customer Analysis Form		Customer _____					
Salesperson _____		Address _____					
Products _____		_____ Telephone number _____					
_____		Buy class new buy straight re-buy modified re-buy					
Date of analysis _____							
Date of reviews _____ _____ _____ _____ _____							

Member of Decision Making Unit (DMU)	Production	Sales & Marketing	Research & Development	Finance & Accounts	Purchasing	Data Processing	Other
Buy Phase Name							
1 Recognizes need or problem and works out general solution							
2 Works out characteristics and quantity of what is needed							
3 Prepares detailed specification							
4 Searches for and locates potential sources of supply							
5 Analyses and evaluates tenders, plans, products							
6 Selects supplier							
7 Places order							
8 Checks and tests products							

Factors for consideration	1 price 2 performance 3 availability	4 back-up service 5 reliability of supplier 6 other users' experience	7 guarantees and warranties 8 payment terms, credit or discount 9 other, eg. past purchases, prestige, image, etc.

SOURCE Adapted from J. Robinson, C.W. Farris and Y. Wind, Industrial *Buying and Creative Marketing*, Allyn and Bacon

3 *The complexity of the product* – the more complex the service offered, the more technical the implications which have to be understood within the client company. Several specialist managers might be required to give their approval before the transaction can be completed.

All those involved in the buying decision are known as the decision-making unit (DMU), and it is important for the key account manager to identify the DMU in the customer company.

According to a *Harvard Business Review* article in 2017 by Toman, Adamson and Gomez,[2] the average number of people involved in B2B purchases has climbed from 5.4 two years ago to 6.8 today. They come from a lengthening roster of roles, functions and geographies. Our advice would be to understand the customer's purchase journey deeply, identifying the most significant challenge at each buying stage.

A useful way of anticipating who would be involved in the decision-making processes in a company is to consider the sales transaction from the buyer's point of view. It has been recognized that the process can be split into a number of distinct steps known as 'buy phases'. These buy phases will be followed in most cases, particularly for major purchases. It will be obvious that at stages beyond the *cooperative* key account management (KAM) stage, the incumbent supplier will have an inside track and, hence, an advantage, throughout the process. In many cases, customers do not even bother to put their proposed purchase requirements out to tender, preferring to deal with their current trusted partner.

Buy phases

This section of the text owes much to the original research conducted by the Marketing Science Institute in the USA under the guidance of Patrick J. Robinson. To read more of his work, see his 1967 publication.[3]

1 *Problem identification* – a problem is identified or anticipated and a general solution worked out. For example, the marketing department finds that it has inadequate information about sales records and costs. It needs better information to be made available.

2 *Problem definition* – the problem is examined in more detail in order to grasp the dimensions and, hence, the nature of the ultimate choice of solution. Taking our earlier example of the international chemical company further, investigation showed that the supplier's original software system was not devised with the customer's current marketing requirements in mind. A new system was required which could also provide the option for the inclusion of other new data.

3 *Solution specification* – the various technical requirements are listed and a sum of money is allocated to cover the cost of investing in new software.

4 *Search* – a search is made for potential suppliers, in this case those with the capability of devising a 'tailor-made' system to meet the above requirements.

5 *Assessment* – proposals from interested suppliers are assessed and evaluated.

6 *Selection* – a supplier is selected and final details are probably negotiated prior to the next step.

7 *Agreement* – a contract/agreement is signed.

8 *Monitoring* – the service is monitored in terms of meeting installation deadlines and performance claims.

> If we happened to be running a computer programming service to industry, we could deduce from the buying process that the DMU at this company might well contain the following people: a marketing planner; a sales director; a sales office manager; the company computer specialist; the company accountant; the company secretary; and perhaps even the managing director, depending on the nature of the contract and the buyer. Sometimes the buyer might be one of those already listed and not exist as a separate role.

We could also speculate with some certainty that each of these people would need to be satisfied about different aspects of the efficiency of our service and we would need to plan accordingly.

For now, it is enough to recognize that, when selling to an organization, the person with the title of buyer is often unable to make important decisions on their own. Although they can be a useful cog in the company's purchasing machine, they are often not a free agent.

Buy classes

Whether or not the account manager is selling to an individual or to an organization, the decision-making processes of the prospects can be divided into what are termed 'buy classes'. There are three types of **buy class**:

1 *New buy* – in effect, all the foregoing discussion has focused on the new buy category. It is here that those people who make up the DMU are fully exercised as the buy phases unfold. In the new buy class, the needs of all decision-makers must be met and influenced by the key account manager. Not surprisingly, this takes time and so it is not unusual for a lengthy period to elapse between the initial discussion and contract closure.

2 *Straight re-buy* – once the salesperson has had the opportunity of demonstrating how the service can help the customer, further purchases of the service do not generally require such a rigorous examination of all of the buy phases. In fact, should the customer merely want a repeat purchase of the same service, their only concerns are likely to be about issues such as whether the price has been held to the same level as before, whether the standard of the service has changed and whether it can be provided at a specific time. Such issues can generally be resolved by negotiation with the buyer.

3 *Modified re-buy* – sometimes a modification of the product or service might be necessary. It might be that the supplier wants to update the product or service and provide better performance by using different methods or equipment. Alternatively, it could be that the customer calls for some form of modification from the original purchase. Whatever the origin, all or some of the buy phases will have to be re-examined and again the key account manager will have to meet with and persuade and satisfy the relevant members of the DMU.

There are often advantages for an account manager in trying to change a straight re-buy into a modified re-buy. They are twofold:

1 A modified re-buy reactivates and strengthens the relationship with the various members of the customer's DMU.

2 The more closely a supplier can match its service to the customer's needs (and remember, this matching only comes about as a result of mutual learning, as communication and trust develop between the supplier and the customer), the more committed the customer becomes to the product or service.

The higher the commitment the customer has to the particular product or service and the supplier, the more difficult it becomes for competitors to break in.

Identifying the decision-maker

Recognizing that there is a DMU is an important first step for the account manager but, having done this, it is essential to identify who actually has the power to authorize the purchase. No matter how persuasive the arguments for buying your service, if you are not reaching the key decision-maker, all your efforts could well be in vain. Identifying this person is too important to be left to chance, and yet many account managers fail to meet with them. Sometimes they just have not done enough research about the company to obtain an accurate picture of its character and key concerns. It is important that the account manager researches the company sufficiently in order to obtain a thorough understanding of its operations, personnel and priorities.

Alternatively, many account managers prefer to continue liaising with their original contacts in the client company, the ones with whom they feel comfortable and have come to regard as friends, rather than to extend their network to include more influential customer representatives. Because many purchase decision-makers will hold senior positions, the thought of meeting them somehow seems a daunting prospect, particularly to complacent or ill-prepared account managers.

Yet many of these fears are groundless. There is no evidence that senior executives set out to be deliberately obstructive or use meetings to expose the account manager's possible inadequacies. In fact, quite the opposite appears to be true. Certainly, the decision-makers will be busy people and so will want discussion to be to the point and relevant. At the same time, they will be trying to get the best deal for their company and it is only natural that they should.

Principal customer contacts/relationships

Draw conclusions about how the customer goes about buying its products and services.

Table 8.4   Template to assess supplier roles and relationships

Name	Title/ function	Role in relationship with supplier	Level of relationship with supplier	Level of importance to supplier

Stage of inter-company relationship overall

Figure 8.10 Mapping the customer

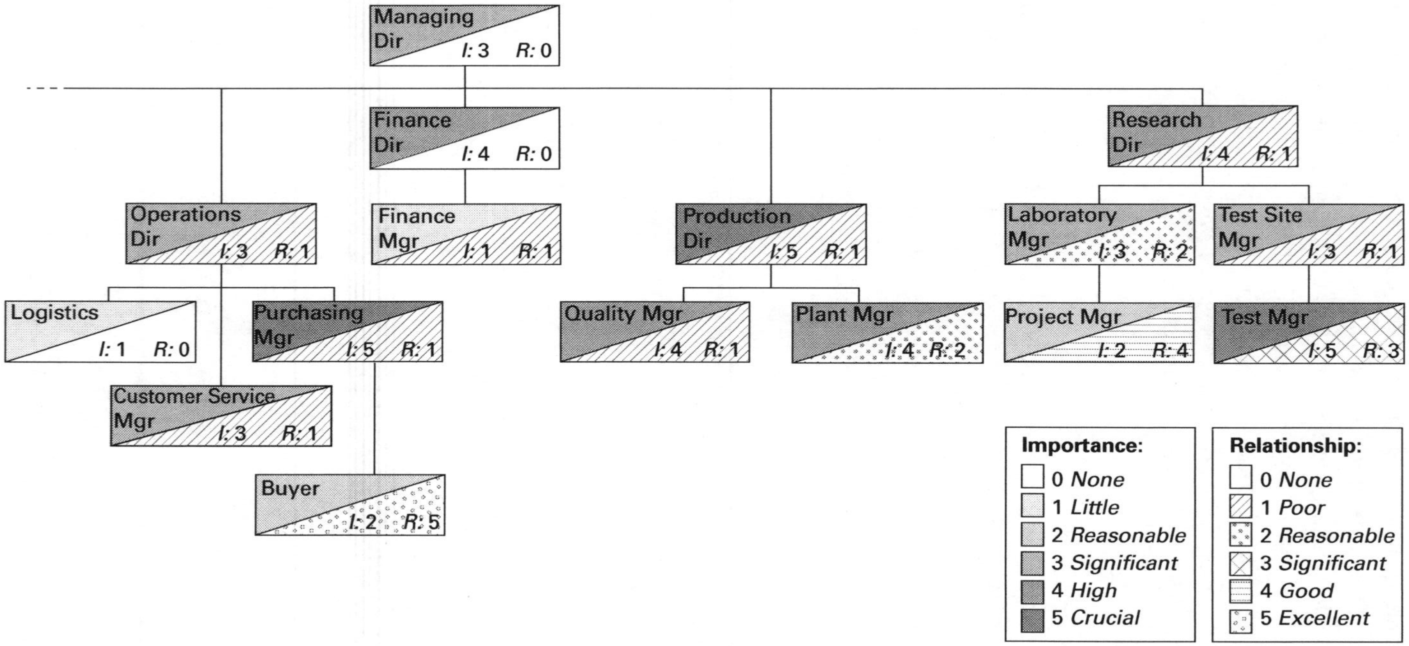

There is, however, one more crucially important piece of analysis to do as part of Step 7. Look at Figure 8.10 and you will see a 'map' of people in the customer's organization structure who might influence what is purchased. You should attempt to draw a map like this for your customer, together with each person's importance and the current level of relationship. It is an easy step from there to set objectives for improving these relationships to the desired level.

For a key, see Table 8.5.

By way of summarizing this section, it is crucial to understand the following:

- the relative influence of the buyer in the context of the particular product or service being offered;
- what constitutes the DMU in the buying company;
- how the buying process works;
- what categories of information each person in the DMU needs to influence their recommendation.

Now attempt to complete Figure 8.9 for a major customer. Exactly how this information should be used will be covered later in the chapter.

Step 8: your sales history with the client

Table 8.6A is a very simple analysis of your sales over a designated period of time working with the customer. The purpose is merely to summarize your business history, share and prospects with this customer.

Step 9: competitive comparison and competitor strategy

Table 8.6B sets out a simple way to compare yourself with competitors.

Figure 8.11, a tool celebrated in a number of my books, shows another possible way of establishing how well you are meeting the customer's needs in comparison with your competitors. It is obviously better if this is done using evidence obtained from independent market research, but provided the analysis suggested in this chapter is carried out thoroughly and with diligence, it should be possible to complete this part of the analysis internally with sufficient accuracy.

Table 8.5 Example of mapping relationship and importance levels

Relationship levels		Importance levels	
The relationship reflected here is that between the supplier as a company and the individual in the customer. Individuals within the supplier may have good or bad personal relationships with each person, but that is not what this table captures. Record the customer's view, even if it includes legacy opinions which you may regard as no longer valid.		The level of importance recorded here should refect the level of importance of this person in the development of the relationship with the supplier.	
Level:	You/others in your company have:	Level	**In developing supplier relationships, this person:**
0	Never met this person, and they would know very little about us.	0	**Is irrelevant**
1	Just an acquaintance with this person OR this person has a very poor opinion of us and/or vice versa.	1	**Has no influence or control**
2	Some dealings with each other, but not consistently, and we do not have anything more than a basic relationship OR this person has opinions about us which inhibit our relationship with them.	2	**Has influence/control over their own personal relationship with providers**
3	A reasonable understanding and a satisfactory working relationship with this person, but it does not extend to the exchange of confidences or special assistance.	3	**Has influence/control over a defined group within the organization**

(continued)

Table 8.5 (*Continued*)

Relationship levels		Importance levels	
4	A good relationship, and work very well together. We are well disposed towards each other and reflect that to our own companies.	4	**Has a strong influence in the overall direction of the organization**
5	**An excellent working relationship; we trust each other and have a high opinion of each other. We are good friends and go out of our way to help each other.**	5	**The most/one of the most important/influential person(s) in the organization**

Table 8.6A Competitive comparison and competitor strategy

Competitive comparison						
	Importance rating	You	Competitor 1	2	3	Implications
Product quality						
Product range						
Availability						
Delivery						
Price/discounts						
Terms						
Sales support						
Promotion support						
Other						

Table 8.6B   Competitive comparison and competitor strategy

Competitors' strategy	
Competitor	**Strategy**
1	
2	
3	

Key:

Importance rating	Rating
(by customer)	(customer view)
A – very important (essential)	1 – consistently/fully meets needs
B – important (desirable)	2 – meets needs inconsistently
C – low importance	3 – fails to meet needs

Guidelines for completing Figure 8.11

Step 1: Select a key account and describe a specific part of this customer's business and the specific product(s) that your company do/could supply.

Step 2: Specify the customer's critical success factors. In other words, what criteria does the customer use when selecting suppliers?

Step 3: Specify how relatively important each of these factors are to the customer (weighting).

Step 4: Score your company and at least two major competitors out of 10 on each of these critical success factors (CSF). Multiply the score for each CSF by the weighting and arrive at a total score for your company and the two selected competitors.

Step 5: Draw conclusions.

The main point of course is that any organization hoping to get and keep business with a major account needs to provide superior customer value and this can only be achieved by comparisons with the best that competitors have to offer.

Please note that exactly the same process shown in Figure 8.11 can be used to analyse *segment* needs as opposed to key account needs. This analysis should be completed for all segments for which you intend to develop value propositions.

Figure 8.11 Strategic management planning exercise – SWOT analysis for a key account

Key account management business strengths – SWOT analysis

1. KEY ACCOUNT DESCRIPTION

It should be a *specific* part of the business and should be *very important* to your company

2. CRITICAL SUCCESS FACTORS

In other words, how does this customer select its suppliers?

1
2
3
4
5

3. WEIGHTING

(How important is each of these CSFs? Score out of 100)

Total 100

4. STRENGTHS/WEAKNESSES ANALYSIS

How would your customers score you and each of your main competitors out of 10 on each of the CSFs?

Multiply the score by the weight.

	You	Comp A	Comp B	Comp C	Comp D
1					
2					
3					
4					
5					
Total score					

5. OPPORTUNITIES/THREATS

What are the few things outside their direct control that have had, and will have, an impact on this part of their business?

OPPORTUNITIES

1
2
3
4
5

THREATS

6. In what specific ways can your company help the customer to deal with the key issues it faces?

Next steps

The painstaking key account analysis is now complete and a number of customer critical success factors will have been accumulated, together with specific ways in which your products or services and processes can help.

Table 8.7 describes a useful way of categorizing your business solutions and approaches to your customer prior to producing a strategic marketing plan for your customer.

The applications portfolio comprises four quadrants. The quadrants at the bottom left and right are labelled 'avoiding disadvantage'. While the meaning of this label might be self-evident, it is nonetheless worth providing an example of this category.

Take, for instance, a bank considering buying automatic teller machines (ATMs) for use by customers outside bank opening hours. Not having ATMs would clearly place the bank at a disadvantage. However, having them does not give the bank any advantage either. The majority of commercial transactions fall into this category.

The bottom left quadrant represents key operational activities, such as basic accounting, manufacturing and distribution systems. The bottom right quadrant might include activities such as presentation material for internal presentations.

In contrast, the top two quadrants represent a real opportunity for differentiating your organization's offering by creating advantage for the customer. The top right quadrant might be beta testing a product, service or process prior to making a major investment in launching it for the customer.

Table 8.7 The applications portfolio analysis

	Strategic	**High potential**
Creating advantage		
Avoiding disadvantage		
	Key operational	Support

Key:
- **Strategic** = issues that will ensure the customer's long-term success.
- **High potential** = issues that, while not crucial currently, could potentially lead to 'differential' advantage for the customer.
- **Key operational** = issues that, unless solved reasonably quickly, could lead to disadvantage for the customer.
- **Support** = issues that, while of a non-urgent nature such as information availability, nonetheless need to be solved to avoid disadvantage for the customer.

This latter point cannot be stressed enough. The whole point of gathering so much information about your key account is to work out ways in which you as the supplier can create advantage for your customer. Anything else is likely to be decided on price.

Mini case 2: gaining advantage

A classic example of a high-potential application was Thompson's computer systems in the leisure/holiday market, where the company was able to place its own holidays at the head of all travel agents' lists.

The reality of commercial life is that most of what any organization does falls into the avoiding disadvantage category. However, leading companies adopt a proactive business approach. They work hard at developing products, services and processes designed to deliver advantage for their major accounts, for it is clear that creative customer-focused suppliers will always be preferred over those who merely offer 'me too' products and trade only on price.

The KAM Best Practice Research Club at Cranfield has strong evidence to suggest that, once such an audit on a key account has been completed, if it is presented formally to senior managers in the account, the response is extremely favourable and, further, that additional confidential information is likely to be provided by the customer to enable the supplier to prepare even more powerful value propositions.

Finally, referring back to Figure 8.2, repeated overleaf as Figure 8.12, it will be clear that all this data and information collected using the tools described in this chapter (described as 'CSFs' in Figure 8.11) can be used to populate the templates as a precursor to developing value propositions.

Summary

Research at Cranfield School of Management has shown that those organizations which invest resources in detailed analysis of the needs and processes of their key accounts fare much better in building long-term profitable

Figure 8.12 Business partnership process

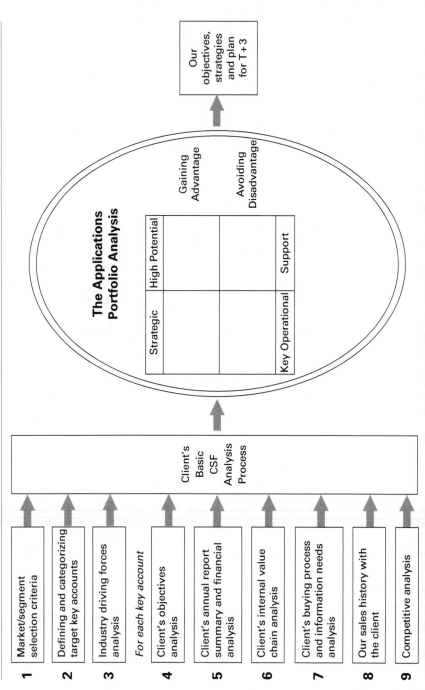

relationships. Armed with a detailed knowledge of your customer's business, it is more likely that you can discover ways of helping them create advantages in their marketplace.

Actions

Please do as much of the analysis as you can, using the templates from this chapter.

References

1 Porter, M (1980) *Competitive Strategy*, Free Press, New York.
2 Toman, N, Adamson, B and Gomez, C (2017) The new sales imperative, *Harvard Business Review*, pp 118–25. Available at: https://hbr.org/2017/03/the-new-sales-imperative [Last accessed 12 January 2018].
3 Robinson, P, Faris, C and Wind, Y (1967) *Industrial Buying and Creative Marketing*, Allyn & Bacon, Boston.

Understanding our own asset base and capabilities 09

Introduction

The purpose of this short chapter is to manage expectations as a supplier. There are obviously lots of promises we could make as part of our value propositions, but as suppliers we need to understand very clearly the implications of the promises we are making.

Take, for example, the classic promise to be 'on time in full' (OTIF). Yet few companies appreciate the costs incurred in making promises like this and the awful financial consequences.

Look at Figure 9.1. This summarizes a survey in a supplier's order pattern over a period of time, with the smallest order size being 500 units and the largest 10,000, with an average of 5,000 and a standard deviation of 100. If this supplier were to keep 5,000 units in stock, they would be out of stock for 50 per cent of the time – clearly unacceptable. If, say, they moved to one standard deviation, they would be out of stock only 18 per cent of the time. Two standard deviations mean about 5 per cent. Three standard deviations would mean about 2 per cent, etc, etc. The problem with this is that at these higher levels, huge amounts of stock need to be made available to guarantee such high levels of service.

The implications are shown in Figure 9.2, which shows that the cost of holding inventory grows exponentially at high levels of customer service, while the response rate doesn't. In other words, at very high levels of customer service, customers don't really notice and take it for granted. This is a classic way to increase costs for little or no return (the costs associated with inventory are shown in the box on the following page).

Figure 9.1   Survey of customer order levels

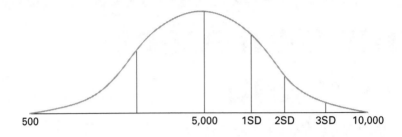

Figure 9.2   The cost of holding inventory

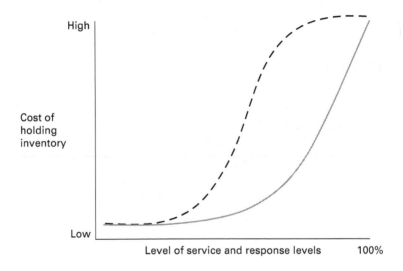

The true cost of inventory

- cost of capital;
- storage and handling;
- obsolescence;
- damage and deterioration;
- pilferage/shrinkage;
- insurance;
- management costs.

Adapted from *Marketing Planning* by Malcolm McDonald (2016).[1]

Figure 9.3   Logistics impact on ROI

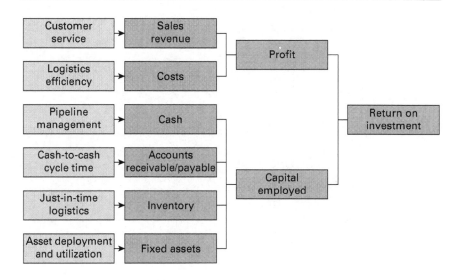

For any accountants reading this book – and we hope there are! – Figure 9.3 shows the impact of this on ROI.

A case history of a value proposition from a commodity supplier

At this point it might be appropriate to introduce one of our favourite case histories, the purpose of which is twofold: first, to indicate the difference between truly strategic and non-strategic purchases; and second, to show how it is possible to make non-strategic purposes more valuable to customers. Figure 9.4 shows the breakdown of purchases by category of a major aerospace company, recently used in my 2016 book *Marketing Planning*.[2]

Almost 30 per cent of its purchases are strategic and clearly much attention will be paid to these. Table 9.1 shows their reasoning about non-strategic items at one stage of their history.

Figure 9.5 shows their reasoning about the perceived riskiness of different types of purchases, with low-value raw materials and items such as stationery being the lowest risk. Their revised thinking, however, occurred when an accountant worked out that it is easy to spend £10 to buy a £1 item – see Figure 9.6.

Figure 9.4   2005 UK spend analysis by segment

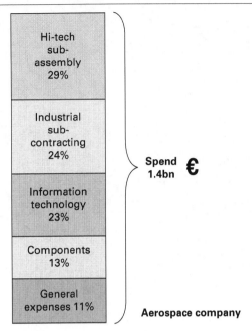

Table 9.1   Strategic versus non-strategic

Strategic	Non-strategic
What purchasing should be focusing in on, the added value items High value production, upstream processes	Can be negotiated centrally Why do people need to negotiate a better price for these items? Where is the added value? For example, general expensed items
It is important to categorize your purchases	

Figure 9.5   Where is e-procurement being used?

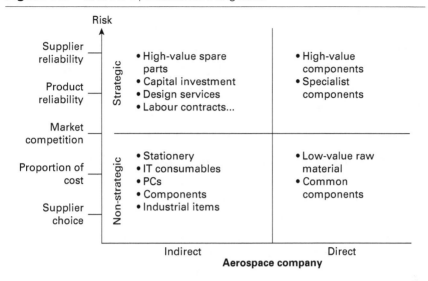

Risk

Supplier reliability ──

Strategic
- High-value spare parts
- Capital investment
- Design services
- Labour contracts...

- High-value components
- Specialist components

Product reliability ──

Market competition ──

Proportion of cost ──

Non-strategic
- Stationery
- IT consumables
- PCs
- Components
- Industrial items

- Low-value raw material
- Common components

Supplier choice ──

Indirect   Direct
Aerospace company

Figure 9.6   The real cost of purchasing items

PLUS PURCHASE COSTS Sourcing Ordering Progressing Responding Staff	*PLUS* STOCK Space Working capital Write-offs Obsolescence M.O.Qs
PLUS OPERATIONS COSTS Purchasing Goods inwards Receiving inspection Handling Stores in/out Kitting Prepping Line feed Etc.	*PLUS* FINANCE Purchase ledger Accounts payable Error resolution

Item cost — Real cost

Do not just consider the price consider the overall cost of doing business with the supplier

'It's easy to spend £10 to procure a £1 item'

Don't forget
Stationery
Equipment: printers, etc
Postage

Aerospace company

It was at this point that an enterprising supplier offered to take full responsibility for the supply and availability of all these low-value commodity items, so saving the customer lots of hassle and cost, at the same time as increasing its own margins substantially – a perfect example of a financially quantified value proposition for a supplier of commodities, and yes, they did use the information in Figure 9.6 to show by how much the customer would be better off by outsourcing the management of all of this low-value stuff.

Understanding our own capabilities

In Chapter 8 we set out how to understand the needs of major customers and of customers within segments.

If you recall, in relation to segments, the SWOT analysis was set out as a great way to understand the needs of customers in segments, as it showed the relative importance of the buyer's critical success factors (CSFs), together with your own capabilities compared with your competitors. At the very least, this showed in what ways you need to improve your offer to win the customer's support.

In respect of major customers, however, the equation is much more complex, because although we now understand customers' needs, we also need to consider whether we are capable of satisfying them better than our competitors.

Here, we recommend that you read the following section on competitive strategies, where I have enlisted the help of an extract from my 2016 book *Marketing Planning*.[3]

Competitive strategies and how to beat bigger competitors

At this point, let me interrupt the flow of this chapter to tell you a story to illustrate what I suspect you already know – how to beat your competitors.

Imagine three tribes on a small island fighting each other because resources are scarce. One tribe decides to move to a larger adjacent island, sets up camp, and is followed eventually by the other two, who also set up their own separate camps. At first it is a struggle to establish themselves, but eventually they begin to occupy increasing parts of the island, until many years later, they begin to fight again over adjacent land. The more innovative tribal chief, ie the one who was first to move to the new island, sits down with his senior warriors and ponders what to do, since none are very keen to move to yet another island. They decide that the only two options are:

1 Attack and go relentlessly for the enemy's territory.
2 Settle for a smaller part of the island and build an impregnable fortress in it (see Figure 9.7).

Figure 9.7   Options for strategy

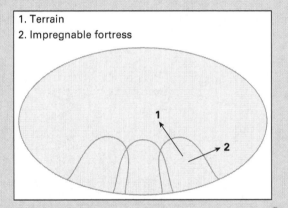

Let's look in turn at each of these options. Continuing for a moment longer with the military analogy, and starting with terrain, imagine two armies facing each other on a field of battle (the soldiers depicted by circles). One army has 15 soldiers in it, the other 12. Imagine also that they face each other with rifles and all fire one shot at the other at the same time; they don't all aim at the same soldier! Figure 9.8 depicts the progress of each side in disposing of the other. It will be seen that after only three volleys, the army on the right has only one soldier remaining, while the army on the left, with eight soldiers remaining, is still a viable fighting unit.

One interesting fact about this story is that the effect observed here is geometric rather than arithmetic, and is a perfect demonstration of the effect of size and what happens when all things are equal except size. The parallel in industry, of course, is market share.

All things being equal, a company with a larger market share than another should win when competing against a smaller competitor. Or *should* it? Clearly, this is not inevitable, provided the smaller company takes

Figure 9.8   The importance of market share

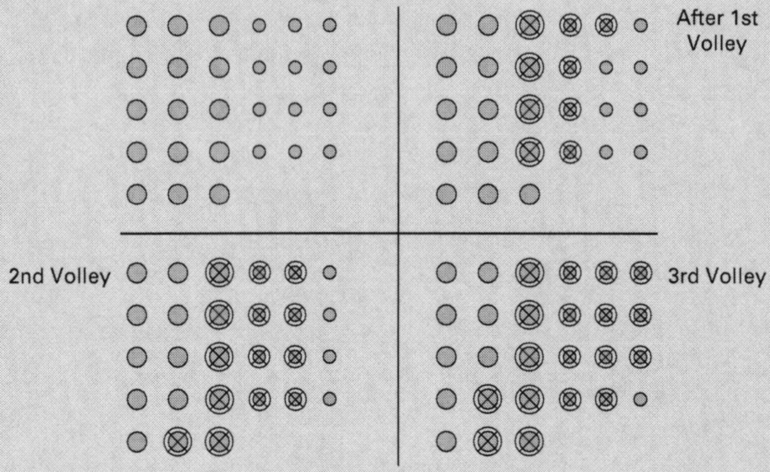

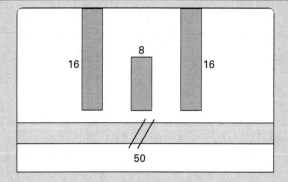

Figure 9.9   The 'David and Goliath' story

evasive action. Even better, small companies can successfully attack much larger ones, especially given the power that technology has given to SMEs.

The David and Goliath story is repeated every day in the 21st century. In summary, Nelson won a famous 'David and Goliath' victory at the Battle of Trafalgar over an enemy with superior numbers. Let's say that the enemy had 50 ships against Nelson's 40 ships. What Nelson did was to split his ships into two groups of 16 and one of 8. The 8 ships attacked the centre of the 50 so that Nelson's 32 ships could attack the enemy's 25. They then re-joined what was left of their own 8 and finished off the enemy.

Yes, of course, this is a highly fictional and romanticized version of what really happened. Nonetheless, it does prove that it is possible to beat a numerically superior enemy with fewer resources. Here are some very general guidelines to help you think about competitive strategies:

1 Know the terrain on which you are fighting (the market).

2 Know the resources of your enemies (competitive analysis).

3 Do something with determination that the enemy isn't expecting.

In respect of this last one, the great historian of military strategy, Lanchester, put forward the following equation when applying his findings to industry:

$$\text{Fighting strength} = \text{weapon efficiency} \times (\text{number of troops})^2$$

Let us simplify and summarize this. 'Weapon efficiency' can be elements such as advertising, the sales force, the quality of your products, and so on; '(number of troops)^2' is more difficult to explain, but is similar in concept to Einstein's theory of critical mass:

$$\text{Energy} = \text{mass (velocity of light)}^2$$
$$E = mc^2$$

Let us take as an example the use of the sales force. If your competitor's salesperson calls on an outlet, say, twice a month for six months, they will have called 12 times. If your salesperson calls four times a month for six months, they will have called 24 times. What Lanchester's Square Law says, however, is that the *effect* is considerably more than twice that of your competitor.

An example of this was the very small competitor Canada Dry attack on the British mixer market. By training the sales force to a high peak of effectiveness (weapon efficiency), and by focusing on specific market segments and out-calling their much larger rival, they were gradually able to occupy particular parts of the market and then move on to the next, until eventually they gained a significant market share. What would have been foolhardy would have been to tackle Schweppes, the market leader, head on in a major battle. The result would have been similar to the fate of the troops in the Charge of the Light Brigade.

Competitive analysis

The greater a competitor's influence over others, the greater their ability to implement their own independent strategies, hence the more successful they are. It is suggested that you should also classify each of your main competitors according to one of the classifications in the guide to competitive position classifications, below, ie leadership, strong, favourable, tenable, and weak (complete Table 9.2).

Also list their principal products or services. Next, list each major competitor's business direction and current strategies. There follows a list of business directions and business strategies as guidelines. Next, list their major strengths and weaknesses.

The guidelines in the box below are useful.

Guide to competitive position classifications

Leadership
- has a major influence on the performance or behaviour of others

Strong
- has a wide choice of strategies
- is able to adopt an independent strategy without endangering their short-term position
- has low vulnerability to competitors' action

Favourable
- exploits specific competitive strengths, often in a product/market niche
- has more than average opportunity to improve their position; has several strategies available

Tenable
- their performance justifies continuation in business

Weak
- currently has an unsatisfactory performance and significant competitive weakness
- they must improve or withdraw

Table 9.2 Competitor analysis

Competitor analysis					
Main competitor	Product/ markets	Business direction and current objectives and strategies	Strengths	Weaknesses	Competitive position

The following box includes five business directions that are appropriate for almost any business. Select those that best summarize the competitor's strategy.

Business directions

1 **Enter** – to allocate resources to a new business area. Consideration should include building from prevailing company or division strengths, exploiting related opportunities and defending against perceived threats. This may involve creating a new industry.

2 **Improve** – to apply strategies that will significantly improve the competitive position of the business. Often, this requires thoughtful product/market segmentation.

3 **Maintain** – to maintain one's competitive position. Aggressive strategies may be required, although a defensive posture may also be assumed. Product/market position is maintained, often in a niche.

4 *Harvest* – to relinquish intentionally competitive position, emphasizing short-term profit and cash flow, but not necessarily at the risk of losing the business in the short term. Often, this entails consolidating or reducing various aspects of the business to create higher performance for that which remains.

5 *Exit* – to divest a business because of its weak competitive position, or because the cost of staying in it is prohibitive and the risk associated with improving its position is too high.

Actions

Consider the competitive strategies example given in this chapter and decide when in your market you may be able to make them work.

References

1 McDonald, M (2016) *Malcolm McDonald on Marketing Planning*, Kogan Page, London.

2 Ibid.

3 Ibid.

Developing value propositions 10

Introduction

This chapter is in two sections. The first section briefly addresses setting value propositions for segments. The second, principal section, addresses the setting and financial quantification of value propositions for major customers.

Section 1: value propositions for segments

It will be recalled that in Chapter 8 we explained how to understand the needs of key segments using a quantified SWOT analysis. The point of a SWOT analysis on each important segment is to spell out quantitatively how customers in each segment choose (critical success factors – CSFs) and the relative importance of each CSF in the decision about what to buy (see Figure 10.1, which shows columns 1, 2, 3 and 4 of Chapter 8's diagram). In such cases, the value proposition cannot be communicated to an individual consumer, but has to be communicated via a whole host of communication channels.

Figure 10.2 spells out the sales process from beginning to end along the top and outlines the kinds of communication channels available to the supplier down the side.

Tables 10.1 and 10.2 are anonymized versions of a travel agency with 10 different segments of customers. Only two are shown here, but they indicate the inefficiency of not understanding the *actual* communication behaviours and preferences of each segment. The message is clear: if you understand the preferences of people in different segments, you will be able to communicate your value propositions clearly and effectively rather than spreading your messages across some mythical average customer, missing your target by a mile and, worst of all, wasting considerable sums of money in the process.

Figure 10.1 Value proposition SWOT analysis

1. SEGMENT DESCRIPTION
It should be a *specific* part of the business and should be *very important* to the organisation

2. CRITICAL SUCCESS FACTORS
In other words, how do customers choose?

1	
2	
3	
4	
5	

3. WEIGHTING
(How important is each of these CSFs? Score out of 100)

Total 100	

4. STRENGTHS/WEAKNESSES ANALYSIS
How would your customers score you and each of your main competitors out of 10 on each of the CSFs?
Multiply the score by the weight.

	You	Comp A	Comp B	Comp C	Comp D
1					
2					
3					
4					
5					
.					

Figure 10.2 Activities by medium

| | Activity | | | | |
	Recognize potential	*Initiate dialogue*	*Exchange information*	*Negotiate/ tailor*	*Commit*
Personal contact					
Direct mail					
Telephone					
Advertising					
Electronic					

Medium (vertical axis label)

Table 10.1 The sun worshippers

	Internet	Mobile telephone	iTV	Broadcast TV	Traditional channels
• Recognize exchange potential					
• Initiate dialogue					
• Exchange information					
Negotiate/tailor					
Commit					
• Exchange value					
• Monitor					

Table 10.2 John and Mary Lively

	Internet	Mobile telephone	iTV	Broadcast TV	Traditional channels
• Recognize exchange potential				■	■
				■	
• Initiate dialogue		■			
• Exchange information		■			
Negotiate/tailor					
↓					
Commit					
					■
		■			
↓		■		■	
• Exchange value		■			
• Monitor		■		■	
		■			

What a segment value proposition might look like

Here is a short case study previously featured in *Malcolm McDonald on Marketing Planning* (2016),[1] but a great example surrounding the impact of the 2008 recession; the number of children being sent to independent schools declined, subsequently along with sales. The knee-jerk reaction was to lower pricing, which led to the whole sector becoming unprofitable. The five factors identified from a study workshop on these independent schools were easily turned into segments: academic, school–family relationships, convenience, cash, and enhancement. Parents wanted a variation on each of these. These factors are listed here.

Figure 10.3 Independent schools

Five critical success factors:

- academic;
- school/family relationships;
- convenience;

- costs;
- enhancement.

Academic factors:

- personality and vision of the headteacher;
- exam results;
- class size;
- league table position (compared with regional competitors);
- student academic successes (Oxbridge, major universities, competitions);
- academic planning: A-level, IB, pre-U, IGCSE? New subjects?;
- flexibility of subject choice;
- academic history (results over a number of years);
- quality, knowledge, experience of staff;
- facilities for teaching and learning;
- learning opportunities outside mainstream subjects (could be vocational skills);
- reporting procedures;
- innovations in teaching and learning.

Figure 10.4   Enhancement/attractiveness factors

- Facilities
    - **buildings and grounds**;
    - **specialist facilities** (floodlit AstroTurf, ICT centre, theatre);
    - **development planning**: plans for new/better facilities.
- People
    - **quality of staff** (teaching and specialist – ie sports/music coaching);
    - quality of staff recruitment;
    - front of house/customer focus;
    - **understanding/delivery of mission** by all staff;
    - strong **alumni association**;
    - active **parents' association**.
- 'Preparation for life'
    - active **careers department**;
    - expertise in **university entrance support**;
    - **work experience, Young Enterprise**, Duke of Edinburgh's Award, Sports Leader's Award, etc.

- Community
    - **links** through activities (charity fundraising, visits to elderly, working with disabled, etc);
    - **hire of facilities** (pool, theatre, sports hall for weddings and parties);
    - compliant with **Charities Act**;
    - **local reputation**.
- International links and opportunities
    - language visits;
    - trips and expeditions;
    - other learning opportunities.
- Technology
    - up-to-date, campus-use access;
    - resources online to enhance study.
- Environmental
    - clear policy and aims;
    - strong **student involvement in campaigns and issues**;
    - clear **priority status** within school – put into action.

Figure 10.5   Relationship factors

- Pastoral care
    - **welfare:** support, information, training, awareness;
    - responsiveness;
    - **structures**;
    - **policies:** availability, clarity.
- Ethos
    - **missions, values**;
    - tangible, delivered from top–down.
- Parents' association
- Alumni association
- Communications
    - internet, intranet;
    - events;
    - printed communications;
    - policies and procedures;
    - management of problems.

Figure 10.6 Cost factors

- Fees
  - fee increases year to year.
- Scholarships
  - type? (sports, academic, all round, music, art);
  - % discount.
- Bursaries
  - % range;
  - means testing.
- Sibling discounts
- Transport costs
- Trips, other extra costs on the bill
- Price relative to regional competitors.

Figure 10.7 Promotional factors

- media coverage;
- stance on current educational issues;
- brand strength and recognition;
- printed materials, information;
- online information and support;
- front-of-house performance;
- events;
- word-of-mouth recommendations;
- feeder school links.

Each school attending this workshop then easily identified nine segments from the detail generated. Two examples are 'academic, results-driven parents'; and 'cost and relationship-driven parents'. The schools then took each identified segment and the five CSFs from Figure 10.1 above, scoring them and weighting them, and multiplied the score by the weight for their own school and at least one competitor.

Not surprisingly, their weighted scores were higher in one or two segments and lower in others, largely because of the nature of the school and its asset base. As an important aside, it was okay to write in column 2 of Figure 10.1, for example, 'academic factors', because behind this there was a deep understanding of what this really meant, given the details of Figure 10.4.

This process is not just for large enterprises, as these schools show. More importantly, however, it enabled each independent school to consider its asset base and develop value propositions for those segments to which they were most likely to appeal.

Taking this all into account, a value proposition for one of the lesser-known independent schools might look as follows:

> We have small class sizes and specially trained teachers so that your child receives personal skilled attention to all their needs. Our facilities provide a wonderful learning environment that will produce results way beyond your expectations. We are renowned for preparing children to face up to the realities of life and to overcome all their fears so that they can compete with those who attend more expensive schools. Our parents' association and alumni bodies are designed to produce a close and loving community to which we are all proud to belong. We are also pleased with the scheme that grants discounts to siblings, as this enhances the family pride of belonging to our community that we all love so much.
>
> We are a small school, but our facilities are in excellent condition and provide a perfect platform for all our children, whether they are of a more athletic bent or of a more academic bent.
>
> We provide all of this at a price which is affordable to those parents who cannot consider the larger, better-known schools.

Before this workshop, the schools were mainly promoting themselves to the whole market with little differentiation and without understanding how to tailor their value propositions to different segments. For example, 'wealthy executives', one of the segments, cared more about life-enhancement opportunities than costs, whereas another segment, 'prosperous professionals', who travel a lot, cared more about costs and maintaining close relationships with the school. The above example of a value proposition was developed for this segment, with much success. As you can see, this tailored form of value proposition is likely to have higher appeal to this particular segment of parents, rather than those in other schools.

After this workshop, our colleague Edmund Bradford developed the successful marketing simulation, which continues to be a great way to practise developing value propositions.

We now move on to Section 2, which deals with the development of financially quantified value propositions for major customers.

Section 2: value propositions for key accounts

You will have understood that if you are to be successful, there is an awful lot of preparation necessary. The following section will therefore help you:

- target those key accounts where you are most likely to get the best results (see Chapter 6);
- list the macro-environmental challenges and issues confronting your key customers (see Chapter 8, Table 8.1);
- summarize Porter's five forces analysis (using Table 8.2);
- summarize the customer's annual report (Figure 8.6) and the financial challenges facing them (Figure 8.7);
- **most importantly,** summarize the customer's value chain (Table 8.3);
- identify the customer's buying process, completing Figure 8.12.

Providing you have been through this process and made notes as you proceeded, you are now ready to prepare your financially quantified value propositions. We are glad to offer you our unique summary of all the foregoing. Table 10.3 summarizes all the analysis carried out in Chapter 8.

Table 10.4 is the most important one in this book, drawing together everything on financially quantified value propositions for key accounts as a result of Porter's value chain analysis.

The final piece

Before presenting your financially quantified value propositions to your customer, there is one last piece of work to be done. Remember, you will need to classify them according to the structure given in Table 10.5.

This is because not all financially quantified value propositions have the same immediate value, and if you are able to categorize them and present them like this, you will stand a much better chance of being listened to and, more importantly, understood.

In conclusion

We know that we have taken you through a long and, on occasions, complicated journey, but please believe us when we say that it will be worth all

Table 10.3 Financially quantified value proposition: workshop summary part 1

Customer's opportunities and threats	Describe the opportunities or threats to the customer	Describe the opportunity for us (the supplier)	Importance to the customer or impact (high/ medium/low)	Added value + ($ € £)	Cost reduction ($ € £)	Cost avoidance ($ € £)	Intangible benefits ($ € £)
From the STEEP analysis							
From the Porter's five forces analysis							
From the annual report summary							
From the financial analysis							
			Subtotal:				

TOTAL: **$ € £**

Table 10.4 Financially quantified value propositions: workshop summary part 2

Customer's value chain weaknesses and opportunities for the supplier to add value		Customer weaknesses	Describe in words the opportunity for us (the supplier)	Importance to the customer or impact (high/med/low)	Added value ($ € £)	Cost reduction ($ € £)	Cost avoidance ($ € £)	Intangible benefits ($ € £)
VALUE CHAIN	Inbound							
	Operations							
	Outbound							
	Marketing and sales							
	Customer service							
VALUE CHAIN FIRM INFRASTRUCTURE	Finance							
	Procurement							
	Technology development							
	HR management							
	Other (e.g. CSR)							
			Subtotal:					

TOTAL: $ € £

Table 10.5 Summary of value propositions

	Strategic	High potential
Creating advantage		
Avoiding disadvantage		
	Key operational	Support

Key:
- **Strategic** = issues that will ensure the customer's long-term success.
- **High potential** = issues that, while not crucial currently, could potentially lead to 'differential' advantage for the customer.
- **Key operational** = issues that, unless solved reasonably quickly, could lead to disadvantage for the customer.
- **Support** = issues that, while of a non-urgent nature such as information availability, nonetheless need to be solved to avoid disadvantage for the customer.

the effort. The good news is that a lot of what we have set out so far has diagnostic processes at its heart, so by following the logic, you are able to carry out a lot of the work independently. We are now pleased to offer you some fantastic real-world case histories in the following chapters, representing the major transformational impact that value propositions have on the enterprise.

Reference

1 McDonald, M (2016) *Malcolm McDonald on Marketing Planning*, Kogan Page, London.

Creating and financially quantifying value propositions

11

DES EVANS former CEO at MAN Truck and Bus UK Ltd

An introduction from the authors

This chapter is a vital component of the book, translating the theory into practice via a case history. This one in particular is an outstanding example of how the profitability of a whole industry, from manufacturers through to channels of distribution and through to the end user, can be significantly improved via financially quantified value propositions. It illustrates that the process is not easy, but also that the rewards to all stakeholders (including society) are significant.

At the beginning of this book it was suggested that those who would benefit most from the concept of developing financially quantified value propositions are those struggling to differentiate themselves. Unfortunately for many organizations, particularly in business-to-business (B2B) markets, this is all too true.

When launching new products, many companies focus on the product features and benefits, the technical specifications and end up as another 'me too' vanilla product, which often becomes commoditized and ends up in a price war with its competitors. The two important questions to be asked, therefore, when developing a new value proposition are:

- Who are your target markets?
- What is your differential advantage?

These are very simple questions but invariably very difficult for many organizations to answer.

We are delighted to receive this contribution from Des Evans, former CEO at MAN Truck and Bus UK Ltd, particularly for the potential influence it will have on persuading you how much impact the topic of financially quantified value propositions can really have to your business. Des received an OBE for services to the transport industry and this case study is but one small part of his massive contribution to an industry that was traditionally working on low margins, particularly due to huge waste and inefficiency.

A case study contribution about MAN Truck and Bus UK Ltd: delivering value and communicating value

The following case history looks at the UK commercial vehicle market over a 40-year period from the 1970s to 2010 and highlights how MAN Trucks, a relative newcomer to the UK market, launched a new product range into a declining market with remarkable results.

The company achieved its goal of reaching 12 per cent market share and selling 6,000 units by carefully selecting its target market and demonstrating a sustainable degree of differentiation from its competitors. Details of how these two key questions were answered will be dealt with later in this chapter, but first it is important to understand the background to how the market had evolved over the 40-year period.

It is interesting to note that the market leadership changed every 10 years and the cause of this was that the primary strategy was production-led and failed to notice what customers really needed and wanted.

The following timeline indicates the changes in both annual sales and market leadership from 1970–2010.

- 1970 UK market > 6 tonnes c.70,000 units – market leader Bedford;
- 1980 UK market > 6 tonnes c.60,000 units – market leader Ford;
- 1990 UK market > 6 tonnes c.50,000 units – market leader Leyland DAF;
- 2010 UK market > 6 tonnes c.<30,000 units – market leader DAF.

The UK commercial vehicle market has experienced tremendous change over the last 40 years. Legislation, emission standards, new technology, foreign competition and the banking crisis have combined to such an extent that by 2010 the annual sales volume had shrunk from a high of 70,000 units in the 1970s to less than 30,000 units.

More worryingly, as far as UK manufacturers are concerned, over 30 UK commercial vehicle manufacturers have gone out of business during this period to be replaced by just seven European brands owned by five organizations.

Bedford, Ford and Leyland trucks dominated the market for over 30 years, but during the late 1970s and early 1980s the Swedish brands of Volvo and Scania together with Mercedes Benz from Germany and DAF from Holland entered the UK market.

These four European brands brought with them not only new hardware but also very attractive value propositions that were not available from the 'home' manufacturers. Volvo and Scania provided more stylish vehicles that were very well equipped with sleeper cabs and night heaters. This appealed very much to the drivers, especially as transcontinental transport from the UK to the Middle East was emerging. Mercedes Benz and DAF supplied similarly equipped vehicles but they added value through the availability of European-wide service stations that supported transcontinental traffic.

Consequently, the British makes of Bedford, Ford and Leyland very quickly disappeared, and today, in a market almost half of the volume of the 1970s, the UK market is the 'home market' for DAF, Volvo and Scania. In fact, nearly 60 per cent of the UK market is made up of these three leading brands.

Against this competitive background UK manufacturers failed to adapt to the new customer needs and focused on product-led 'business as usual'. In addition, the transport business model was also changing with the growth of the 'white van man' and the significant increases in the van population, with annual sales increasing from 150,000 units to over 300,000 units.

The development of the internet and home delivery business models would further add to the truck manufacturers' misery; however, it also opened up the opportunity for a whole new value proposition to be presented to the UK transport marketplace.

Answering question 1: who are the target markets?

Against this background of market volume decline, an example of a new customer value proposition in the UK truck market was developed by MAN

Truck and Bus UK Ltd, a wholly owned subsidiary of the German MAN Group of companies.

MAN are a famous German engineering company who celebrated their 250th anniversary in 2008 with the statement:

MAN – Engineering the future since 1758.

Amongst their most notable achievements is the invention of the diesel engine, developed by the engineer Rudolph Diesel, who was contracted to the MAN company from 1893–97.

The MAN diesel engine has for many years been the means of differentiation from other brands because of its reputation for reliability, ease of maintenance and good fuel consumption, but, as with many engineering-led companies over the last 20–30 years, good basic engineered products are no longer enough.

The customers demand more than good engineering and, more importantly, even good engineering can be copied and sold on price alone. Look what happened to Bedford Trucks and Ford Motor Company!

On 24 March 2000, the MAN Truck Company launched its latest generation of heavy commercial vehicles: the TGA, or the Trucknology Generation to give it its full marketing description (see Figure 11.1).

TRUCKNOLOGY by MAN Trucks – 'It's not about the Truck!' was the start of introducing a new value proposition that was based on a service strategy that helped transport operators better control their costs with the introduction of telematics.

Its target market was operators within a 30-mile radius of the 70 UK workshops, as research had highlighted that truck operators were not prepared to travel further than 30 miles to the nearest dealer.

Figure 11.1   The TGA Trucknology Generation

Answering question 2: what is your differential advantage?

The TGA range represented a new type of product insofar as the vehicle now incorporated electronic, digital components compared with the traditional analogue, mechanical vehicles that dominated the marketplace.

The new product also introduced the concept of 'Trucknology'. Essentially, this brought together knowledge of both the trucks and transport industries. The production of this new range had taken place over seven years and at a cost of over €1 billion. However, the electronic, digital nature of the product enabled a whole new value proposition to be created and delivered to the customer. In the UK a number of key customers were consulted and their views of what truck manufacturers should be supplying were discussed and taken seriously. The main points raised were that the overriding concerns of the operator were not really about the product. Many of the comments were along the lines of, 'all trucks are the same', 'it's only about the price'.

The real concerns of the operators, however, were the cost of fuel, the performance of their drivers and the service and maintenance schedules in order to keep the vehicles on the road with the minimum downtime. Fuel and uptime were therefore highlighted as critical success factors as far as the launch of this new model was concerned.

It was further noted that the transport operator's profitability was also a major concern, with average return on sales of 3–4 per cent. For a 44-tonne articulated unit travelling 150,000 kilometres per annum, this meant that bottom-line profitability would be £5,000–£6,000 per vehicle per annum. This represented a relatively very low return for a high-risk operation.

In addition, in terms of uptime, with vehicle availability for 300 days per annum, a 3 per cent ROS meant that for 291 days the truck operated for nothing. Profitability was only secured in the last 9 days of the year, and that was on the assumption that no other unscheduled downtime was incurred!

Understanding the total value chain

Figure 11.2 highlights the total operating cost and income of a typical 44-tonne articulated vehicle travelling 150,000 kilometres per annum. What is interesting to note is that the actual 'product cost' is only 10 per cent of total annual cost. Fuel and driver costs represent over 70 per cent, and it is the management of these costs that are important to the customer.

With this in mind, a customer value proposition was developed that would focus on helping the customer better control the operating cost by

Figure 11.2   Total cost of ownership – profit and loss account of a typical haulier

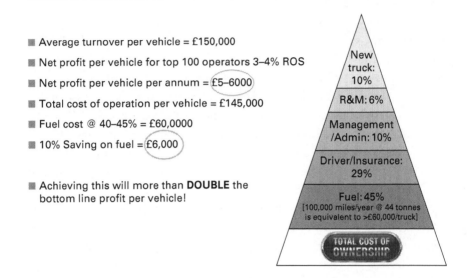

- Average turnover per vehicle = £150,000
- Net profit per vehicle for top 100 operators 3–4% ROS
- Net profit per vehicle per annum = £5–6000
- Total cost of operation per vehicle = £145,000
- Fuel cost @ 40–45% = £60,0000
- 10% Saving on fuel = £6,000

- Achieving this will more than **DOUBLE** the bottom line profit per vehicle!

New truck: 10%

R&M: 6%

Management /Admin: 10%

Driver/Insurance: 29%

Fuel: 45%
[100,000 miles/year @ 44 tonnes is equivalent to >£60,000/truck]

TOTAL COST OF OWNERSHIP

providing real-time management reports that managed fuel consumption and driver performance.

Delivering and communicating value

In its marketing communication (see Figure 11.3), 'the product' was referred to as the tip of the iceberg and the real danger was the 90 per cent of invisible costs that were below the waterline. It was these costs that the TGA range, as a result of incorporating telematics into the service contract offer, was able to support the operator in a way that provided a unique market offer that the competition were unable, until later, to match.

This value proposition was further validated by the results of monitoring 1,000 drivers who travelled over 3 million kilometres during a pre-launch research study. The telematics data showed very clearly the need for driver training, when 90 per cent of the 1,000 drivers examined in the research were shown to be not operating at benchmark (B) performance levels.

What was more important was that the ability to operate at benchmark performance levels would yield a 10 per cent reduction in fuel consumption, which would in turn DOUBLE the bottom line of the typical operator (see Figures 11.4 and 11.5).

Using the Energy Saver A–G ratings, the average driver performance was rated as a D. When the fuel consumption of a D driver was compared with that of a benchmark B driver, the difference in consumption was 11 per cent.

Figure 11.3 MAN's customer focus – focusing on operators' whole-life costs

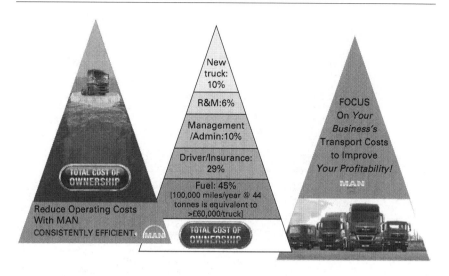

Figure 11.4 Driver categories as tested – >1,000 UK tractor drivers tested

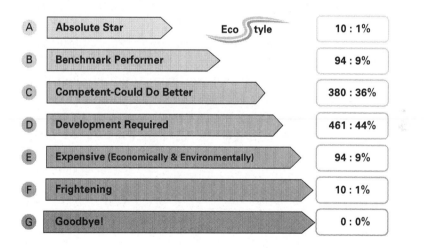

This research led to the creation of a value proposition that highlighted the need to focus on the total cost of operation as opposed to the traditional bargaining on the price of the product. This sounds like a very simple message to communicate, but it had serious implications for both the sales and service networks as it represented a need for significant change to the traditional way of working.

Delivery and communication of this new TRUCKNOLOGY concept was further developed with the aid of the internet and the introduction of the

Figure 11.5   Fuel consumption

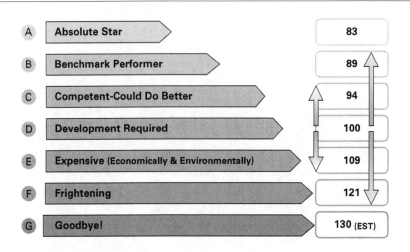

A	Absolute Star	83
B	Benchmark Performer	89
C	Competent-Could Do Better	94
D	Development Required	100
E	Expensive (Economically & Environmentally)	109
F	Frightening	121
G	Goodbye!	130 (EST)

www.trucknology.co.uk website, which enabled operators to connect with both MAN and its dealer network.

Together with the development of the website, a new business solutions approach to the market was introduced that enabled customers to track the performance of their vehicle in real time and for the service organization to arrange service schedules online and provide the customers with an electronic archive of all important legal documentation. This was a very significant development in service capability that further differentiated the brand from the competition.

A new franchise proposition, the UTP programme, focused on providing the customer with a guaranteed uptime and ensured that any vehicle called in for service would be back on the road within 24 hours. This development led to the creation of a further added value service called Mobile 24, which managed all roadside breakdowns and again gave MAN a leading position in the supply of national service cover.

Figures 11.6 and 11.7 show the three online solutions developed with Trucknology Fleet Management:

1 document management system – electronic service documentation;

2 transport management solutions – vehicle and driver performance;

3 dealer workshop management – service scheduler and technician control.

This new Trucknology offer to customers soon started to show results.

Figure 11.6 MAN website screenshot 1

Figure 11.7 MAN fleet management

Quantifying value for all stakeholders in the value chain

Operators with the typical 3–4 per cent ROS saw their bottom lines improve significantly as drivers improved their performance. Increased profitability also led to more enlightened operators establishing incentive schemes for drivers to earn their share of the increased profitability. Further operator cost savings were delivered in the form of tyre wear, accident damage and reduced insurance premiums and this resulted in significantly improved customer satisfaction levels.

The Heavy Truck Study of 2010 (see Figure 11.8) highlights the development of customer retention over a five-year period, 2006–10. The MAN TGA range performance significantly improved over this period. A 42 per cent rating in 2006 moved to a 75 per cent rating in 2010. More importantly, the company moved from a bottom-of-the-table seventh position to a podium second place finish in 2010.

This development took place over a five-year period and highlights the need for consistency of message and how long it takes for an organization

Figure 11.8 HTS 2010 – UK customer retention, aftersales index of customer retention

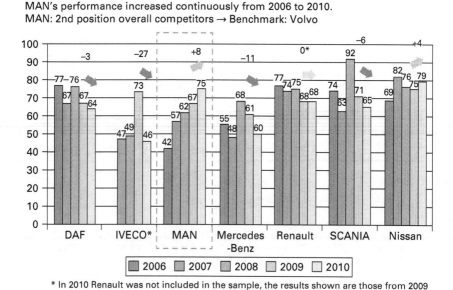

MAN's performance increased continuously from 2006 to 2010.
MAN: 2nd position overall competitors → Benchmark: Volvo

* In 2010 Renault was not included in the sample, the results shown are those from 2009

to bring about business model change. It is not easy, but it can be achieved if the appropriate internal communication and culture is created.

Conclusions and lessons learned

Changing a traditional business model that is considered to be standard practice in a conservative industry is extremely difficult and should not be undertaken lightly. The launch of new, electronic, digital products, however, allows organizations to seriously consider their current routes to market and addresses the two key questions facing many company executives:

- What are your target markets?
- What are your sources of differential advantage?

In considering any radical business model change, the following five issues should be clearly understood.

1 *Assess the state of company readiness* – for the executives who have the 'big idea' for change, do not make the mistake of assuming the rest of the organization will follow you. Change will be resisted, particularly by those areas of the organization that fear that their current positions and departments will be threatened.

   There are many examples of new product launch failure due to the customers having been told one thing only for something else to be delivered.

2 *Internal communication before external communication* – in order to reduce the level of resistance to change, it is important to develop clear, consistent INTERNAL communication BEFORE any EXTERNAL information is delivered to customers. The external market will only be convinced of the new value proposition if the customer-facing staff have total belief in the new way of working.

3 *Establish a clear value proposition* – the value proposition needs to be clearly understood and this has consequences for the internal organization and associated networks. Product-led organizations sometimes struggle with the concept of lifetime value, especially when this becomes the basis of differentiation. This issue may have consequences for training and skills development and requires an assessment of core competences and resource capacity.

4 *Understand the risk* – developing a new customer value proposition and changing the business model is not without risk. There is a risk that the new customer offer costs more to deliver than is first calculated. There is the risk that the process of delivery or execution is flawed. Early testing with valued key accounts can eliminate many errors and actually increase customer intimacy.

5 *Establish and agree operating standards* – any value proposition carries with it roles and responsibilities.

This is especially the case with advanced services that guarantee outcomes. It is therefore important to establish basic standards of operation and clearly communicate what the customer's role and responsibilities will be in ensuring the required outcome.

Final comments

The MAN Truck and Bus UK case study shows that a relatively small commercial vehicle importer can compete with the home market competitors at a time of enormous industry change. Table 11.1 shows the development over the period 1992–2012.

Market share increased fourfold from 3 per cent to 12 per cent, turnover increased by a factor of 12, parts sales increased from £10 million to £100 million, and with over 10,000 vehicles under contract, a new future contract income of approximately £250 million was created.

In addition, many truck operators are now operating more profitably and the dealer network with a new service-based franchise proposition has seen the ROS change from 1 per cent to 6 per cent, albeit on smaller turnovers.

Table 11.1   MAN in the UK, 1992–2012

Market share	3%–12%
Turnover	£50m–£600m
Vehicle sales new and used	1,500–8,000 pa.
Parts sales	£10m–£100m
50% of sales with finance and service contract	
10,000 units under service/fleet management	

The average dealer now has a service turnover of £4 million with a 6 per cent ROS (£240,000 per annum) compared with a previous sales and service turnover of £12 million with a 1 per cent ROS (£120,000 per annum).

A value proposition is therefore not just for the end customer but for all the stakeholders in the value chain, and is proof that with the right internal communication, culture and leadership, a generic company can compete at the highest level.

Developing and presenting value propositions that resonate with customers

12

TODD SNELGROVE former Global Vice President of Value, SKF

An introduction from the authors

Many thanks for this valuable contribution from Todd Snelgrove, former Global Vice President of Value, SKF: helping companies be more profitable by defining and pricing for the value they bring customers.

Todd has played the value evangelist for the past 20 years inside SKF, a global industrial engineering bearing company headquartered in Sweden. He has worked tirelessly to help his company understand and create products and services that truly create customer value. He has developed a systematic, best-in-class approach and methodology to quantify customer value with the SKF Documented Solutions Program, which, at the end of 2017, had over 100,000 cases of approved customer value worth over US$7 billion in hard value. This enabled and positioned the technical and engineering-focused sales force to effectively communicate the value created in monetary terms.

Finally, he has worked on developing guaranteed value agreements with over 135 global customers focused on driving up value for both parties while reducing customers' true costs and making sure both the supplier and customer get an even greater sustainable benefit. An example of this can be seen by SKF winning the 2015 Strategic Account Management

Association Excellence Award for impacting customers' metrics using a joint scorecard. Specifically, the tool, methodology, and process to find, implement and share value resulted in both customer and supplier winning.

The market that SKF is involved in has followed the evolution seen in other industries, in which the technical buyer is losing authority to buy what they want from a person they like, to a procurement focus that says what do we need, what will it do for us, and how much should we pay for it? For those from other industries, be on the lookout, as other markets are following this evolution from technical buyer to commercial buyer, and for them the value proposition of your solutions needs to be tangible, and if you can monetize the value proposition for the customer their willingness to pay, and their ability to pay, for your offering increases.

Todd now supports other companies, in any industry, to put forward the programmes, processes and tools to develop and quantify value propositions that customers are willing and able to pay for value.

Quantifying your value so customers are willing and able to pay for it

This chapter is graciously reprinted with kind permission of Routledge Business Press, from the acknowledged book *Value First Then Price*.[1]

How does one get paid for value created? The question has been asked by every premium player in every market in the world. Given that the financial benefits of value creation, value proposition development, and value pricing are well known, why do so many companies fail to achieve the desired results after they've done the work to create something of value? For those that do invest and create customer value, it's time to do the work to get paid for it!

$$PV \geq COST = ACTION$$

I have begun to look at this as a formula. If the perceived value (PV) of a good or service is greater than or equal to the cost of buying it, an action such as a purchase should occur. In more detail, it is the perceived value from the customer's perspective; however, if that value can be expressed monetarily, it will be a harder value than a perceived value that is not. Cost includes the asking price, plus all other associated costs (shipping and handling, research time, the cost of capital, etc). If I perceive that I will obtain more value than the cost of doing so, it probably will result in a purchase. The greater the difference between perceived value and cost, the higher the percentage of people who will buy. For example, if the quantified customer-specific value is $100, and the cost of acquiring it is $42, a value surplus or incentive to buy of $58 exists, and for most that surplus is large enough to motivate most people toward the desired action of purchasing. However, let's assume that perceived value is a feeling (no number is assigned to it); in this case, fewer people would buy. Finally, if the perceived value were only $43 and the cost were $42, far fewer people would invest in buying to receive the $1 of benefit.

Looking at the example in Table 12.1 of an offering for a tool called a laser alignment system, we see a list of perceived values; let's assume for each item there's a value that, based on industry averages or customer-specific numbers, totals $10,000 and that the total costs of acquiring the tool are $4,200, leaving a value surplus or 'incentivization' benefit of $5,800. If the numbers are a hard value, believable to me as a buyer, I will find a way to get the $4,200. In general, the harder and more monetary the value numbers are, the less value surplus is needed to get an order.

Companies that employ a good value-based pricing strategy are 20 per cent more profitable than those that have weak execution on value pricing, and 36 per cent more profitable than those that are good at executing a cost- or market-share-driven strategy.[2] Thus I would argue that value pricing works only if additional areas are also addressed. A company must create value, communicate that value through sales and marketing, and quantify

Table 12.1 Example of perceived value calculation for a laser alignment tool

Perceived value ≥ costs = action		
Less energy consumption		
Faster installation	Price of tool	
Longer machine life	Cost of adding or using existing vendor	Order or no order
Easier installation	Time to wait for delivery of tool	
Less machine vibration		
$10,000	$4,200	$5,800 value surplus

SOURCE Used with kind permission of Routledge Business Press

that value in monetary terms; only then can it get paid for the value created. Think about it for a second: if a company is great at three of these but not the fourth, it won't get paid for value.

As I travel the world, I hear too often from CEOs the refrain, 'I want our sales force to sell based on value but they do not... why?' The answer is simple. No one size fits all and no silver bullet exists. Selling on value takes focus, management support, tools, and training, and attributes to see the results. In talking with other thought leaders in the value space, I have come to realize that numerous other things need to happen to make value selling work for a company.

For a sales force it comes down to two main focuses: do they have the ability to sell value? And do they want to sell value? I find that most companies focus on the ability area and assume that the sales force wants to sell value and that they just need to go and do it. So what's needed?

Why spend the time and effort to quantify your company's value?

The first step in the journey is to realize that quantifying value is something your customers want and need you to do, something that will allow them to justify buying your option unless you're consistently the lowest-priced offering. In the world of buying and pricing, two competing forces exist. From a customer's perspective, these are the *willingness* to pay for value and the *ability* to pay for that value. In the days when the user of a product or service was the decision-maker, and purchasing was more of a clerical function, the process was easier – easier in the sense that the user of the solution you were offering could justify in their own mind what better, longer, easier, faster meant because they were the ones who would receive the benefit. However, in the last two decades, the activity of 'purchasing' has evolved into the strategic focus of 'procurement'. The difference is important: now procurement decides what is of value, what they are willing to pay for – and because they are not the ones who will see and receive the benefits, they are less likely to pay for them. Second, in today's budget-constrained world, the question is whether the customer has the money or budget to buy the better offering. The case studies, research, and anecdotal stories that follow show that if value can be quantified in the universal language of dollars and cents, obtaining new budgets or reallocating money from another budget can easily happen, and procurement will be willing to invest.

For example, I might say to a potential customer (user of a product or service), 'This solution will allow you to do the job 22 per cent faster, and the quality of the job will be 10 per cent better' (assuming data exist to reinforce this). How willing and able would that customer be to pay for that value? It would depend on what those impacts would mean to them and on comparing this buy with other, competing purchases. They might sense that mine is the better solution, and then they would have to take this argument to their boss, procurement, and finance and explain that time is money, for example. However, what if after mentioning the above benefit statements and, based on industry averages, or their company-specific measurements, I handed them a customized business case showing that my solution would save their company $225,000 a year in overtime, parts, reduced scrap, and less re-work? Which scenario has a better chance of getting the order? Now they would know what the solution was worth and where it would rank with competing requests for the two very scarce resources of time and money. In today's world, where your offering is competing for funding and priority over other options, the one that has the best business case, with the hardest values, and the highest probabilities of realization, will be the offering that is purchased. If you cannot quantify the value of your offering, it will be placed in the dreaded no decision, or low-priority, bucket. Or the purchase will be seen as a commodity and you will be compared with your competitors based on price and delivery. Instances of decision-by-committee have increased, and 'let's not make the wrong decision' seems to be a dominant driving force. It's easy to point to 'we got all the minimum requirements at a lower unit price' to support a bad supplier selection if ultimately things don't work out. However, with a vetted business case, all functions involved in the decision can point to the payback, ROI, and cash flow of the business case provided to justify why that project or solution was approved over the other options. Even when there is no budget, if the payback is believable or guaranteed, money can easily be reallocated or found when a quantified business case exists.

So once you see the need for and benefit of quantifying your value, what else needs to happen to enable your company to sell and get paid for that value? Let's look at the internal and external resources, requirements, and focuses needed (see Figure 12.1). These are not ranked by order of importance; however, you need to address all of them to be truly successful. Over the last decade I have had the chance to sit with the guru of value, Professor James Anderson, and discuss what's working, what's not, and why, in our company's and others' 'value merchant' strategy. After one discussion, Jim created the diagram shown in Figure 12.1. I was amazed at how clearly he was able to represent the main points and show how they support the

Figure 12.1 What causes value-selling success

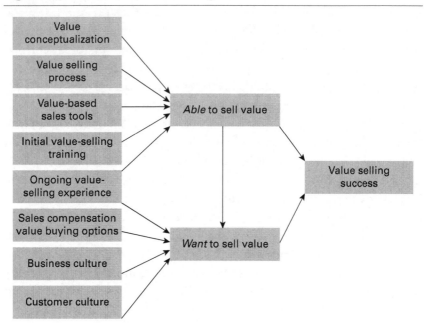

SOURCE   Illustration courtesy of James Anderson (2015). Used with kind permission of Routledge Business Press

two areas of ability and willingness to sell value. Checking to make sure we address all areas listed in this diagram ensures that we cover all the basics for a vital, ongoing, robust programme based on value that allows a company to differentiate its offering from that of the competition.

The 'ability to sell value' component

Value conceptualization

What is your company's value to your customers? What does it help them do better than the other options? Value selling begins with the basic step of making sure your company creates something of value. Whether it's a product or a service, it needs to have an attribute that is not only different but also of value to someone within your target audience. Most academics use the term 'unique selling proposition' or USP; however, just because something is unique doesn't mean it is of value. At our company's 100-year celebration, our CEO took the stage and memorably said, '*Value is not in the minds of our engineers and what we think value is; value is what customers value.*'

Years ago, while interviewing for my job at SKF (a Swedish-headquartered global leader in industrial engineered products), I asked our Canadian president why customers would choose to buy an SKF bearing over a competitor's offering, when we had a price premium. I will never forget the stone-faced glare of our Swedish president, who said – almost in disbelief that I didn't already know why – 'We are Swedish.' I began to chuckle and then realized that he wasn't joking. So, our head office is in one country, whereas our competitors' are in others. This is unique, but it's not something of value (to me, at least). What I heard him say was that our head office is in Sweden. What he meant was that we make the highest-quality products in the world, and that we've generated more innovations and patents than all our competitors (Swedish culture is highly innovative and focused on quality). So the first phase of value selling is to make sure that you create something that is of value to your customers – whatever that may be.

Since publicly traded companies have a shareholder responsibility to create sustained profit, let's make sure we help them do this in the right way by adding real value and taking out real cost. To get buy-in, this value must be quantified.

Value-selling process

Second, value has to be part of your selling process. Are you merely reacting to customers' requests, or are you proactively engaging customers, solving problems, and articulating that value during your sales process? The Corporate Executive Board,[3] a US think tank, recently found that of more than 1,400 B2B customers' sales interactions, those customers completed, on average, nearly 60 per cent of a typical purchasing decision in researching solutions, ranking options, setting requirements, benchmarking pricing, and so forth before they even talked with a supplier. So if the customer has decided that three suppliers meet their minimum criteria, price is the only measurable thing of difference. In this case, it's hard to come in and say, 'Hey, you need to rethink your requirements: what you really need to do is measure value or total cost of ownership.' However, based on experience, we've been able (although it's harder when it's later in the sales cycle) to say, 'Should we be discussing the $5,000,000 in annual parts that you buy and a price savings of 5 per cent on that if you give me an additional $2,000,000 in business ($350,000 theoretical price savings), or the $4,000,000 in CAPEX and OPEX savings (hard EPS improvements) our company can help drive to your bottom line by getting your facilities to a world best-in-class average? An opportunity for profit that is 11.5 times bigger.' All the customer can

Figure 12.2 Total cost of ownership

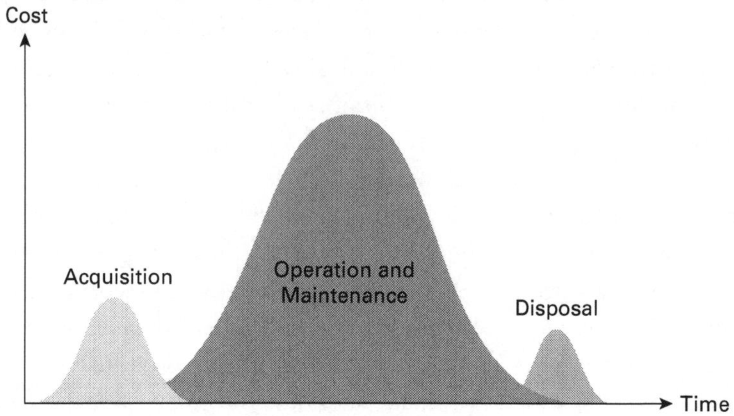

SOURCE Used with kind permission of Routledge Business Press

now ask are questions such as, 'Has this happened before? What's the probability that it will happen? How will we measure it? What happens if you hit or miss your target? What payment relationship should we have?' These all move into the discussion of implementation to realize value.

Can your sales force have an intelligent discussion with procurement, finance, engineering, and even the customer's CEO to explain how lowest price is not the same as lowest cost? Can your company affect, measure, and reduce costs and increase value in using your product or service during the phases of acquisition, installation, operation, maintenance, and disposal? Can your company also increase the benefits your customer receives, such as increased production, reduced risk, increased safety, increased sell-through? By looking at the total cost of ownership (reduction of costs) along with the total benefit of ownership (increase in benefits of value), you can now understand and demonstrate in numbers how you can affect and measure the impact of your offering on their total value of ownership – which is the difference in reduced costs plus increased benefits minus any price increase – thereby making them measurably more profitable (see Figure 12.2).

Value-based sales tools

Most companies mistakenly think that having a value-based sales tool is the Holy Grail and the end of the value journey. As companies have said to me in the past, 'If we just had a methodology to sit down with customers and document for them where and how much more money they can make or save using our offering versus the next best alternative, all our problems would be solved.' This is one of the foundational building blocks; however, it is only part of the journey.

At SKF, in the early 2000s, we realized that all the superior technical benefits in the world of our products wouldn't matter to a VP of finance or procurement unless we could convert what those features and benefits meant into cold, hard cash. With that in mind, we created a tool called Documented Solutions Program™ (see Figure 12.3). It is our methodology for sitting down with the user of the solution and running an expected and eventually an actual business case ROI. This financial justification for the customer can now be used to show their bosses the benefits in hard cash of choosing to work with SKF, or to buy a specific solution. We are not the lowest-price provider in our industry, but we can help customers realize the lowest costs by using our services and products. This tool and methodology has become a mainstay of our business, and each year we report the numbers generated. At the end of 2014, we had over 56,301 accepted or verified cases with customers, with savings of over US$5 billion, covering all five of our technology platforms. You can imagine the power of sitting down with a customer and demonstrating how this same offering has helped their own company at a different location in the world, or someone within the same industry, save so many dollars by implementing this solution. The conversation goes from 'how much does it cost?' to 'when can we get this started so I can start saving money and solving a problem?'

For a value quantification tool to really work, it must be easy for the technical and financial person to understand. Remember, a good TCO tool is not a sales tool in and of itself. It's a process and methodology for benchmarking, finding, prioritizing, customizing, and quantifying expected values in financial terms so that customers can see if it makes sense for them to invest in your solution. Too often I see company-made templates that are really just a sales tool called something else.

Characteristics of a good TCO quantification tool:

1 Benchmarks data ranges and reference points.

2 Allows customers to change input data.

3 Is clear and concise. Sometimes engineers overcomplicate things and think the more detailed, the better.

4 Shows the results as your customer would like to see them, for example in terms of ROI, net present value, cash flow break even, dollars saved.

5 Is functional – allows users to save cases and work through a process to go from proposal, to accepted, to verified.

6 Builds in an archive so that cases can be saved, searched, and sorted by industry, application, country, distributor, customer, and so forth.

7 Provides live updates when connected to corporate server; links to reference material.

8 Is easy to use – available in a light version such as for an iPad (SKF launched in 2015), multiple languages and currencies, and so on.

Initial value-selling training

Now that you know your offering has value, your sales process incorporates value, and you have tools for demonstrating and quantifying value, you'd better make sure your sales force is comfortable with selling based on value versus price or technology. During initial training, spend time discussing why this is a good strategy for them and your company and why customers want and need proof of value. Programmes that come as edicts from the head office usually encounter resistance in the field that is not needed. Bring the team along on the journey; don't ram it down their throats. Of course, they need to understand and practise with the tool's functionality. Also, if your sales force is technical, you will need to spend even more time getting their buy-in. For SKF this has been an issue, because we hire engineers, for whom the technology itself explains the value. They tend to be happier talking about product features and benefits such as the hardness of the steel or the precision of the manufacturing process – and if the solution proves the value, why would one need to convert that value into dollars and cents? When talking to other engineers, they're right; they understand what these things mean – but finance does not. Over the years, we've launched and used a great outside global sales consulting group to ensure that our teams feel comfortable with and know how to sell based on value, and that they're comfortable with terms like return on investment, return on equity, net present value, and how we affect a customer's earnings per share. If your sales force doesn't understand these terms or know how your company's offering can affect your customer's profit, some training is required.

In the ability-to-sell-value stages we focused on the basic underpinnings needed. Next we discuss what else needs to happen to keep the culture change programme alive and thriving with your team, and with your customers.

Figure 12.3 SKF documented solutions

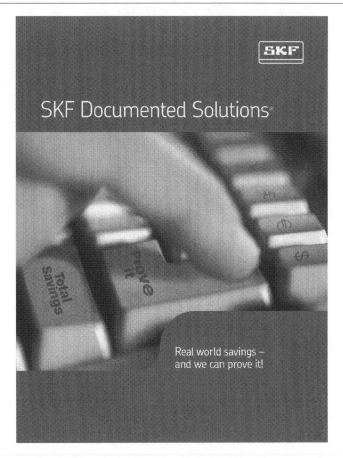

SKF Documented Solutions®

Real world savings – and we can prove it!

SOURCE Used with kind permission of SKF and Routledge Business Press

The 'want to sell value' component

Ongoing value-selling experience

However, training is not a one-and-done thing; it must be ongoing. Just as athletes train daily, so should salespeople. At SKF, we have just begun to do role-playing in which a senior manager acts as the customer and challenges our salesperson's presentation and offering and asks, 'What's the value for me, the customer?' You will only be good at and comfortable with value selling when you know and have answered similar questions hundreds of times. What will procurement's response to this offer be? Let's practise and think through what their possible objections might be so that we're prepared on game day. I also like regions and countries of the world that include the discussion of value during every meeting, where someone presents a case, what numbers were used, how the process worked, and key learnings. Having regional experts to do joint sales calls with, along with management drive-along and coaching, must be ongoing, and part of an annual reminder of the importance and focus of this initiative within your company.

Sales compensation and value buying options

If you can prove value, companies can pay for it. Sales compensation will have an impact on how your people behave. Do you incentivize volume targets? If so, you shouldn't have to ask yourself why your salespeople are so eager to cut prices. In some organizations I have seen sales targets set as a threshold, with no consideration of whether a deal was struck by providing discounts. Some companies might think of themselves as advanced because they reduce the sales amount to the net discounted price. However, for a company with a 10 per cent net profit margin, a 5 per cent price cut is the equivalent of realizing only half the profit dollars. Also, remember that free services, free samples, free training, extended terms, and so on are just other, more creative ways for a salesperson to discount your offering. I suggest that the salesperson who sells less but at full price should be rewarded more than the salesperson who spends most of their time with management justifying that a particular customer needs to get a discount.

We've looked at how you pay your salespeople, but we should also look at whether you've given your customers an option to buy based on value realized. In other words, do you use pay-for-performance models that allow customers to pay once value is realized for them? If not, they might not be able to buy based on promises of potential future value. At SKF we use a few different methodologies: for large customers we might enter into a guarantee of annual cost savings. As a CEO once said to me, 'I have 25 different ways to offer a discount, such as volume, competitive issues, industry, new business, et cetera, but I don't have a way to guarantee the value we create … that has to get fixed.'

It's great to offer customers value, but have you offered them ways to pay for that value that fit their particular situation? Before moving on, let's be clear about what it means to get paid for value. It's not about 'extracting' all the incremental value delivered to the customer in a price premium, for example. To do so would leave the customer with no incentive, or value surplus, to incentivize them to choose your option. Second, I believe most companies have a 'buy my product or service at a price' option only. However, a whole set of options needs to exist based on the customer's situation and what

Figure 12.4 Pay for performance options

Most companies are happy to share profit.
SKF Reliability Systems is willing to

share risk.

An alternative to traditional maintenance practices or full outsourcing,
an Integrated Maintenance Solution (IMS) gives SKF Reliability Systems
responsibility for your machine asset management strategy. We share some
of the risk as well as the savings, while you receive agreed upon financial
returns and technology upgrades – without capital investment.

Our on-site team provides the services and support best suited to optimize
your plant's asset efficiency and integrity. All services are delivered under
one fixed-fee, performance-based contract. Also included in the terms is
a guarantee that SKF will pay back part of the contracted fee if agreed
upon goals are not met.

Each agreement is different, customized to your specific business needs,
complementing your internal resources.

Is an IMS agreement right for you? Contact us to discuss your potential ROI,
and to hear some of the results we've produced for other companies.

SKF Reliability Systems
www.skf.com/reliability

SOURCE Used with kind permission of SKF and Routledge Business Press

they value. The extreme is a 'buy my products at a certain list price with a
100 per cent pay-for-performance' option. Within SKF we call this an IMS,
or integrated maintenance service, agreement. As with many outsourcing
agreements, we focus on where we can drive the most immediate customer

savings. So, we might say, 'Mr Customer, what did you pay last year for all the parts, people, and operating expenses to run these factories?' 'X.' 'Okay, we will do it better (measuring these deliverable KPIs and doing it for an immediate savings of Y). However, as we make you more money, we get a reward as those benchmark targets are exceeded (e.g., increased production).' I would say that outsourcing IT in general follows this model, and it can make sense. Corporate experts focused on just information technology delivery should be better at it because it's their core expertise. This is a great offering; however, a few issues could arise, and I have seen companies try this, along with other pay-for-performance agreements. If all the offsets are not listed, something that looks good (increased production, less inventory, etc) might be a short-term win; but if assets are pillaged to do this (they were run with no proactive maintenance), actual losses – not savings – will result. Just think what a pump will really be worth in a few years if the proper maintenance isn't done. All those proposed or even realized savings will be more than offset by increased future costs. With that in mind, pay-for-performance agreements work if they are long term, so that no one is incentivized on such short time frames. However, in between these two options, other getting-paid-for-value formats should exist. A simpler version is, 'Mr Customer, although our products might have a higher average initial price of X, we guarantee an annual hard savings that exceeds this.' The benefit is that the customer is getting value for paying more, and the value becomes ongoing, whereas price reductions are one-time (suppliers won't or can't offer a 5 per cent per year incremental price savings, but they can offer a new 5 per cent guaranteed savings in another area). As a customer, as long as the savings are hard, measurable, and don't force other costs up, I am willing to keep paying more as these savings compound and make me more sustainably profitable.

A question I've been asked by procurement professionals is, 'Which is better: an acquisition price savings or ongoing annual cost savings?'

Imagine you're presented with the following choice: a 5 per cent upfront price savings on a contract for 5 years or a 5 per cent annual cost savings over 5 years (see Figure 12.5). Which is the more valuable option? First, let's assume something that rarely happens – that the 5 per cent price savings will actually make it to your company's bottom line and that no unintended increased costs will occur elsewhere. Let's also assume that the 5 per cent annual TCO savings are real and measurable – lubrication savings, for example.

Given these two scenarios, some procurement people might assert that because both are 5 per cent, they are worth the same. This analysis would

Figure 12.5 5% price versus 5% annual TPA™ improvements?[4]

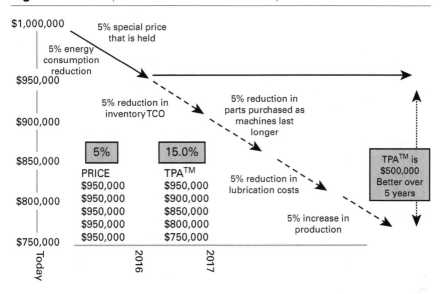

SOURCE Used with kind permission of Routledge Business Press

be correct after year one, but not after year two. Switching to a new supplier may bring a 5 per cent price savings, but that supplier would not offer and would not be able to deliver that incremental price savings every year thereafter.

From a TCO perspective, however, during year two an additional 5 per cent savings would be generated by focusing on a new area of opportunity such as energy savings. The magic of compounding and ongoing annual savings would allow a TCO annual 5 per cent savings to be worth 15 per cent versus the 5 per cent price savings over a five-year period. Remember, we assumed the best-case scenario for the substituted product based on price.

IACCM research shows that a focus on price concessions undermines the value achieved. For example, the probability of a poor outcome increases by more than 50 per cent, compared with agreements that focus on performance. This translates into significant increases in cost and missed or lost revenue – at levels far exceeding the theoretical savings from the low negotiated price. SKF has provided thought leadership in this area for more than 20 years, having successfully resisted 'commoditization' by switching instead to delivering market-differentiating value (Tim Cummins, CEO, International Association of Commercial and Contract Management, quoted in SKF 2014, p 2).[5]

Business culture

Are you really a value company? Does your CEO talk non-stop about the value you create for your customers? Do you reward and recognize the people who create the most value or the newest ways to save customers money? Or are you just using a few buzzwords on a PowerPoint slide or corporate brochure? Value needs to be part of your company's DNA. Does sales get mixed messages like, 'Get every order and sell value'? Unless your message is clear, you will end up rewarding and motivating sales to cut prices, and volume will be the underlying dimension that's rewarded. If you're unable to prove your value, you might get a short-term order based on lowest price, but over time it will not translate into more sustainable orders as someone comes along and undercuts you. We are lucky at SKF to have as our leader a CEO who continually focuses on value as our main differentiation.

Customer culture

Does procurement see you as a commodity and therefore assume you can be bought using certain tactics, or do they see your offering as strategic for them?

As a company you can do all these other things well, but if procurement sees you as a commodity, and buys your product or service as such, much effort needs to be exerted by everyone to get procurement to rethink where and why they have chosen to treat you that way. In my experience, most companies have an issue here. Let's begin with the way procurement chooses how to select suppliers and negotiate with them based on the Kraljic four-box matrix. The Kraljic Matrix (see Figure 12.6) is a well-respected thought process introduced in 1983 in the *Harvard Business Review* article 'Purchasing must become supply chain management'.[6] Although the concept has since been modified (to a 9-box or a 36-box matrix), and procurement's implementation of it has evolved over the years, the thoughts and resulting actions of procurement still follow this concept. Too often there is a mismatch between how we perceive ourselves as sellers and how buyers perceive what we are selling, leading both sides to wonder why they cannot communicate.

A key driver of procurement is to increase spend under management (they control a higher percentage of the company's procurement dollars spent) and to buy from fewer suppliers (to increase leverage and to reduce transaction costs). When I am at a Strategic Account Management Association

Figure 12.6 Kraljic Matrix[7]

	Security	Strategic
Risk/Business Contribution	**Security**	**Strategic**
	Reduce risk	Partnership
	Continuity	Value engineer
	Conformance	Negotiate
	Nuisance	**Leverage**
	Ignore	Leverage
	Automate	Exploit
	Bundle	Switch

Spend

SOURCE Adapted from Kraljic (1983)

(SAMA.org) conference, and I ask senior global strategic account managers, 'Where do you see your company on this matrix?', in general I get the following feedback.

Comments such as, 'We are not the small, unimportant *nuisance* offering, where transaction costs are the most important differentiator.' However, I say, for suppliers in this realm, ease of use and ordering efficiency are the most important characteristics and decision-making criteria for procurement, with unit price being most important. When thinking about size, we need to look at what percentage of the customer's total spend we are. In general, suppliers will focus most of their efforts on direct material spend, as that is where the most money is spent. When companies rank suppliers on spend they tend (of course) to place direct materials (all the products that go into making their primary product – steel, for example) on the right-hand side of the matrix because a small savings on a big number would seem to have a bigger effect on company profit. As we will see, the spend with a supply category is probably not the primary indicator of where efforts should be focused or the biggest hard savings and benefits can be realized. Although the y-axis represents the business contribution, if you cannot quantify the business contribution, procurement will assume that all offerings are the same and will push you into the lower two quadrants.

Most of us are not in the top left quadrant, either, at least not in the long term. This quadrant is where a supplier exists that is not a huge percentage of the customer's total spend but that has a product or service that cannot be easily substituted. Remember, the ease of substitution is based on the customer's assumptions, not ours. If you happen to have a patent on a product or service that they need or access to a chemical or raw material that no one else has, or if demand exceeds supply in a market, you are in this position. However, in general, this is not a long-term realistic position to be in. If what you sell has an ISO specification, competitors are reasonably the same size and offering, and the perceived risk is very low or zero. I recall Rob Maguire saying that people are confused about what an ISO standard is: 'It's a conformance standard... not a performance standard.' Yes, both products are the same size, fit the same hole, and so forth; however, that doesn't mean they'll produce the same results or perform the same way.

We suppliers want to think that we're strategic – that if the customer would really work with us, we could offer a lot of value, savings, benefits, risk reduction, and innovation. Talking with procurement professionals at numerous global conferences over the past decade, I find that they would place none or only a handful of suppliers in the top right quadrant as *strategic*. However, after I discuss how often that's a mistake – that a lot of suppliers could really help their companies be more profitable by doing things differently – the standard retort is, 'Then why don't they come to us and demonstrate and document how they would do that, and what the impact would be?' Sales and procurement functions both need to take responsibility for placing suppliers in the wrong quadrant and therefore not getting the possible or desired results.

The above segmentations are the backbone of a value-selling organization and culture; however, if the customer still perceives that the dollar spend with you is not significant (the x-axis in the Kraljic four-box matrix) and you are not strategic enough to spend the time or effort to treat them like a partner and demonstrate the value you could bring, much of the above won't help. When you get to the procurement person or team at your customer and they are aggregating volume, threatening with low-priced offerings of competitors, contemplating the use of a reverse auction, employing some sort of benchmark pricing that shows, somewhere, one time your product price was less, asking you to explain your cost breakdown to justify a final price, then you should know that your customer sees you in one of the bottom two boxes and will focus on leveraging you. Most people forget that the x-axis label represents financial contribution and they focus on dollars spent instead. This is a major issue that sales needs to address. Our company has made it a focus, and we have people whose job is to get customers to understand that even though the relative dollar spend might be low (versus direct spend such as raw materials), the impact can be huge. I think the x-axis should measure financial opportunity dollars (money saved using existing TCO, or financial improvements total value of ownership). For example, supply risk might be low because other global players exist and products have an ISO specification. Dollars spent is relative. Customers might purchase US$10 million of industrial parts to keep their plants running, but when their total spend is US$5 billion, some might assume that this 'supply bucket' should be treated as non-critical or as a nuisance leverage buy (0.2 per cent... not even close to 1 per cent of total spend). However, when looking at how value can be created by reducing operating machine costs (less energy, water, lubricant, repair parts, labour, and/or increases in machine production, throughput, or quality), one customer saw that our impact could be worth US$128 million in savings. We were then moved immediately to the *strategic* quadrant.

To help the market evolve, you need to do some research, work like a consulting organization that talks about the results you can impact and by how much. Don't just discuss the technical features of your widget. We need procurement around the world to challenge their assumptions. We spend a lot of time at procurement and academic conferences presenting our thoughts and methodology. This has proved very helpful in moving our market to change how they measure and choose suppliers, the most advanced being on hard value generated. A nice reference and study that I use is from Manufacturers Alliance for Productivity and Innovation (2012),[8] a US-based think tank that represents industrial manufacturers. A study they conducted with the procurement representatives of member companies found that companies that had a structured way to buy on best value were 35 per cent more profitable than companies that had no structured methodology for measuring and understanding value.

To keep the programme alive and flourishing

As I have shown in the focuses or requirements needed, a value quantification tool needs to be the output of the strategy of creating, communicating, quantifying, and getting paid for value; however, numerous other issues need to be addressed: 'A fool with a tool is still a fool.' For value quantification to become a company focus, a mantra, a part of who your company is and the reason for your being, other supports must be in place. Some suggestions follow.

Who will drive this programme internally and externally? A programme without a driving person is destined to fail. Barker and Liozu (2013)[9] observed, whenever this question is posed to a group of businesspeople,

'Who's in charge of value in your company?', someone will inevitably shout out, 'Everyone!' Really? If everyone owns something, no one does. Adam Smith demonstrated that the *division and specialization of labour* were a central cause of the wealth of nations; they are also the central cause of the success of a business. Not everyone can be good at everything (p104; italics in original).

Will the ability to quantify the value of new products and services be part of your new product development process, so that when a new 'solution' is presented to the market you can quantify its financial impact for customers?

External marketing should consistently reinforce this as part of your brand image. I'm not a fan of hearing how old a company is, or how big it is, or how many people it employs. What's in it for the customer to buy your company's offering? Spend time on the 'so what is the benefit' and less on the how (the how can be discussed in face-to-face meetings). A tagline of mine is 'Making Industry More Profitable'. I might employ the smartest people, I might be the most knowledgeable, I might have more patents, and I might have the best products... these are just things I can apply to a customer's business, with the result that I make them more profitable. Say what the result is; don't make the customer assume what those benefits will be for them. Trade shows, magazines, brochures, and company speeches should have a dedicated 'section' where your company can summarize the hard value your company has delivered.

The value journey is never-ending; an almost-as-good competitor will always be ready to copy your latest innovation. To stay out of the commodity game, and to make yourself and your customers more profitable, demonstrate and document when, where, why, and how you can affect how much money they make. It's not a zero-sum game if you can quantify your value; then you will be remunerated with an equitable portion of that value.

References

1 Hinterhuber, A and Snelgrove, T (2016) *Value First then Price: Quantifying value in business to business markets from both a buyer and seller's perspective*, Routledge, London, pp 75–90.

2 Monitor Pricing Group (2011), cited in Bertini, M (2011) Profiting when customers choose value over price, *London Business School Review.*

3 CEB (2012) CEB identifies anatomy of the new high performer, 20 December, *PRNewswire/CEB.*

4 Snelgrove, TC (2016) Center for Advanced Procurement Studies Annual Conference, June, Oxford, UK.

5 SKF (2014) *Lowest price ≠ lowest cost: buying on total benefit of ownership boosts profitability by bringing sustainable savings to the bottom line*. SKF White Paper. Available at: http://cdn2.hubspot.net/hubfs/332479/SKF_TCO_TBO_White_Paper.pdf?t=1441284795161 [Last accessed 14 October 2015].

6 Kraljic, P (1983) Purchasing must become supply chain management, *Harvard Business Review*, **61** (5), pp 109–17.

7 Ibid.

8 Manufacturers Alliance for Productivity and Innovation (2012) *Approaches towards Purchasing on Total Cost of Ownership*, A MAPI Council Survey, Arlington, VA.

9 Barker, RJ and Lizou, SM (2013) Who is in charge of value? The emerging role of chief value officer. In A Hinterhuber and S Liozu (eds), *Innovation in Pricing: Contemporary theories and best practices*, Routledge, New York, pp 99–118.

Author biography

The author of this chapter, Todd Snelgrove, now supports other companies in any industry to put the programmes, processes and tools in place to develop and quantify value propositions that customers are willing and able to pay for. He can be reached at todd@expertsinvalue.com or www.expertsinvalue.com

Value-celling: how to maximize value creation in supply chains

13

MARK DAVIES Managing Director of Segment Pulse Limited and Visiting Fellow at Cranfield School of Management

Many thanks indeed for this valuable contribution from Mark Davies, Managing Director of Segment Pulse Limited, Visiting Fellow at Cranfield School of Management and author of *Infinite Value: Accelerating profitable growth through value-based selling* (2017, Bloomsbury Business, an imprint of Bloomsbury Publishing Plc).

What is the chapter about?

Many original equipment manufacturer (OEM) organizations need to get their products and services to end-user customers in increasingly global markets. As a cost-effective solution, they adopt supply chains as a means to achieve this challenge, working with a range of (often) smaller organizations to extend their logistical, commercial, technical and operational reach.

While being cost-effective and flexible, these supply chains can cause problems. With a lack of understanding of value and customer value-proposition, there can be a shift of emphasis from creating value for the end-user customer and fighting for business based on transactions and cost. For the OEM suppliers this can mean that the supply chain destroys value, rather than enhances it.

This chapter looks to discuss a complex supply chain by telling a story. The author has worked within an industry, seeing the perspective as the end-user customer, the OEM supplier and several of the players within the supply chain. Over a 20-year period, Mark Davies has shifted his perspective: initially he was an engineering manager in a pharmaceutical business, and laterally he works as a consultant and researcher for suppliers looking to create and develop strong customer value propositions. Mark tells his story, and then offers a practical way of thinking to enable OEM suppliers to build supply chains that act as 'value-cells' – providing a competitive advantage for all of the players in the supply chain.

Introduction

Most business-to-business organizations serve their customers by supplying products and services through a series of intermediary organizations. This is for a combination of reasons but mainly for cost-efficient distribution that can reach and serve markets on a wide and varied scale. These supply chains are complex, multi-faceted and often specialized groups of industries and organizations – all of which are looking to develop their own successful and profitable futures.

Understanding how supply chains work is a critical skill for any business that is developing an effective strategy. And yet, it is often the case that organizations misunderstand or even totally neglect to consider the critical importance of an effective supply chain. Two reasons might contribute to this lack of focus. First, supply chains are complicated and take some considerable effort to understand. Very few organizations can say that they have total control of the third parties that form the supply chains they utilize across the world, and of course, that is the point. With control comes cost – and that is exactly why firms adopt 'loose' third party supply chains. Second, the concept of value and how value is created and demonstrated between suppliers and customers is often misunderstood. In supply chains, these interactions and exchanges of value (through products, services and solutions) are numerous and occurring on a highly frequent basis.

For organizations that want to maximize the value potential that they can offer to the initial designated 'end-user' customer, life can be frustrating and difficult to manage. It is hard enough for suppliers to shift discussions from price (if they are locked into negotiations with procurement) and to try to realize a higher overall fee based on the real benefits and value that they provide. When they have to trade through several layers of intermediary, while there are obvious essential and logistical benefits that are provided, the value impact for the end-user can become confused, dislocated and significantly diminished.

For many of the firms that I work with when assisting them to develop innovative value propositions and new ways of value-based selling/key account management, it is always sobering to ask these clients a pertinent question. How much of your business goes direct to your target end-user, and how much goes via third parties?

Typically, there is a range of 20 to 60 per cent for most industries whereby the supply chain accounts for the sales and delivery of their offering. I have worked with organizations where this percentage split is much higher, and on some occasions 100 per cent of business flows via third parties. It is vital to consider how the supply chain works in the delivery (and destruction) of your end-user value proposition – and yet it is notoriously tricky.

To explain in a bit more detail how supply chains enable and hinder value creation, I will tell a story that I have been involved in over a 20-year period from three different perspectives. The story looks at the perspective from different players within the supply chain: the end-user customer, the OEM supplier, and supply chain organizations operating between these two.

By reviewing the dynamics and thinking of a supply chain from the perspective of the supplier, a customer and the players within the chain, along with my own value-based business models, I hope to be able to provide a simple model that can be used to analyse and understand how to make supply chains create value most effectively for business marketing organizations seeking to sell their products and services.

A supply chain story

My story starts in 1995. I was the engineering director for a contract pharmaceutical manufacturing company. We had a unique, specialized and patented process, and served our customers by manufacturing unique oral dosage form products. We were part of the supply chain by providing the ethical pharmaceutical organizations (Merck, Pfizer, GSK, etc) with packaged products. It was an exciting time. Our US parent company recognized that there was significant potential in the process and had agreed to make a multi-million-dollar investment in our UK site. This involved new buildings, special-purpose equipment and support utilities.

At this time in the mid-1990s, the US Food and Drug Administration (FDA) were taking a real interest in manufacturing facilities. They looked to the design and specification of the processes and critical support facilities, and wanted to see evidence of approved validation systems and ongoing maintenance and calibration records. Without these things being in place, FDA auditors could fail audit processes and withhold the submission of manufacturing and supply licences. Suddenly the humble engineering department was becoming far more critical an activity, and its actions were under the spotlight of senior management, customer auditors and regulators. Building a new facility was going to be exciting but also very challenging.

Of particular interest was the selection of the systems that would constantly monitor and control the environmental, utilities, security and key processes. Known as a building energy management system (BEMS), this would act as the brain of our new facility. Selecting a reliable and well-developed system would be critical to the future approval of the new facility. As the person in the organization that would be responsible for the design and operation of the facility, I had a real interest regarding the system that we would select. Actually, it was more than just an interest. It was a key responsibility and professional obligation.

In order to select the BEMS provider and the design company that would develop the design and oversee the installation, I had to work with the principal design and build organization that we had selected. They subsequently directed me to the mechanical and electrical contractor who they had subcontracted to oversee the building controls. In building and facility construction, this 'work-package' approach and subcontracting of major activities is normal. It enables competitive bidding to take place, splits down the risk exposure if a contractor goes bust (it is better for a small contractor to fail than a large one) and it enables the main contractor to access a huge breadth and depth of expertise in the marketplace as they invite organizations to bid. My facility had some 32 work packages – the BEMS being just one of them. It was tough to find out who owned the assessment of the system within my own project team, let alone understand how to influence the final selection!

Figure 13.1 shows a simplified supply chain map of how the BEMS provider would get their products to me as the customer (end-user). There are three steps/organizations between us, each one adding value and trying to create value as they are contracted and incentivized, but also working with a relationship that is narrowed, ie supplier and customer. As the end-user customer it took some real effort to be able to get involved with the selection and design influence of the BEMS. For 80 per cent of the overall facility, this was fine – I was happy to discuss concepts and designs with the principal design and build contractor. For things like walls, drains and steelwork, they were the experts and managing these 'commodity' items were best left to them to deal with and achieve the best specification and performance for the best price (this was why they had been chosen as a principal contractor, after all). The selection of the BEMS was absolutely critical and as the ultimate person responsible for its correct usage, I had to get involved and be more accountable.

Figure 13.1   Mapping the supply chain

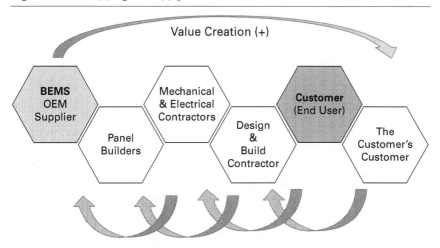

SOURCE Used with kind permission of Bloomsbury Business, an imprint of Bloomsbury Publishing plc

The starting point was to select the BEMS hardware provider. This was done by a series of interviews discussing a high-level brief that we developed. Focusing on pharmaceutical standards, software structure and the ability to discuss the way that the systems were developed was key (since we would have to validate the installations during the final commissioning of the facility testing). We initially looked at the top three market leaders and, following a few weeks of intense discussions, selected the BEMS provider.

The next stage was initially handed back to the mechanical and electrical contractors, as they had to select a panel builder. Of course, this was conducted following the usual bidding selection process. As the end-user, we were also involved with this activity, focusing on technical performance more than price. This created a tension: the usual contractual mechanisms for this activity apparently do not include the end-user. We had to agree and sign off additional costs and fees that would be incurred as we strayed from the exact 'cost-centric' approach favoured by the bid and selection teams. This activity whereby the end-customer got involved in the selection process of both hardware and the installation teams was unusual, but honoured. This overall build went ahead as planned, commissioning and validation of the site took place and we received FDA approval and operated a commercially successful site that was operating 'on time' and within budget.

The second part of the story comes about 15 years after this event. My role was as a consultant and researcher. I was commissioned by the BEMS provider to try to assess the supply chain and evaluate what the various organizations within the chain wanted (they were considering developing commercial/sales training programmes).

I interviewed six of the panel builder organizations, and two contractors. They were all very professional and highly successful organizations, but there was one over-riding conclusion that I derived from the discussions: *nobody within the supply chain was thinking or acting beyond the organization that they were directly contracted to serve.* This meant that the bigger picture and total 'value in use' calculation within this supply chain was fractured and lost. For the players within the supply chain, real value could only be obtained by receiving products that were lower in price (since this would reduce their overall cost and increase their profits).

In itself, there is nothing wrong with this. But for the OEM supplier, it meant that they would always be in a position whereby they were developing a long-term high-quality product that could not have this value fully realized by receiving payment from the end-user customer. Value was being stifled by the supply chain for the OEM supplier, since it was working as a cost-saving process for the constructors within it that operated on short-term building contracts.

I met with a very senior sales director for the OEM supplier and discussed the findings. I also told my story of when I built a site (acting as an end-user customer that worked across the supply chain). Seemingly, the way that I had behaved was very unusual, in fact it almost never happened. In fact, end-user customers were increasingly outsourcing the operation of their sites to facility management organizations, so not only was the construction and specification of equipment severed between OEM supplier and end-user customer, the lifelong operation (where real value could be realized!) was also fractured.

My reflection of this situation was to really consider supply chains and how they create (and destroy) value. This story highlights issues that are common for many organizations in many industries. This chapter looks to discuss the workings of supply chains, and to help OEM suppliers understand and manage value creation more effectively.

Value in business marketing

Any sales conversation in business marketing should focus on the value that is being created for the customer. Failure to understand what the customer needs, and describing your offering in the context of those needs, will potentially shift your discussion from the potential 'value you can create' to the 'price that will have to be paid'. As Warren Buffett famously states, 'Price is what you pay, value is what you get.'

Figure 13.2   The value equation

The (4+1) sources of value impact
- Top line
- Bottom line
- Business reputation and continuity
- Strategy, organizational and advisory
- Meeting consumer needs

Value = | Impact | − | Total Cost of Ownership |

The costs of ownership
- Initial purchase price
- Ongoing costs of operating
- Ongoing costs of 'not operating'

SOURCE Used with kind permission of Bloomsbury Business, an imprint of Bloomsbury Publishing plc

And yet, many organizations (and especially sales people) will have discussions with customers and other supply chain partners without really understanding what it is that the customer values. Instead, they are more concerned with trying to push what it is that they have to sell: their products and brands. Of course, these are the bedrock of what they will provide, but they should always be discussed as a means of providing real value to the customer.

Supply chains, as described in Figure 13.2, are a series of buy–sell relationships. In my BEMS story, value was being fractured for the BEMS supplier because of these separate discussions. In order to comprehend value more accurately, it is worthwhile discussing what value is. Figure 13.2 is the value equation. Value can be stated as a source of impact on the customers' business, less the total cost of ownership.

Value impact comes from five areas:

- *Top line* – adding value to the customers' business by helping them to grow sales and drive the top line of their profit and loss account.

- *Bottom line* – adding value to the customer business by reducing costs in the operation of the way they do business (variable costs) and/or reducing fixed costs. Addressing bottom-line value focuses on the way the customer conducts their business and helps to preserve top-line performance for stronger final profits.

- *Business reputation and continuity* – these are aspects of business that do not feature in the core of the business reporting (sales, costs, fixed and variable assets, etc). Despite being intangible, they have enormous issues for any business. Such things as health, safety, and security, environmental and quality are critical to business reputation and the ability for them to keep trading.

- *Strategy, organizational and advisory* – business today is fast paced and ever-changing. Customers have to respond to changing macro-economic new norms, technology advancements and changing competition. Suppliers can offer significant value to them by providing advice and support to help them navigate through difficult and changing conditions.

- *Meeting consumer needs* – often the final customer is a consumer. If you consider my BEMS example, the consumer would be a patient that would take the pills we manufactured. Understanding how consumers behave and what they value can provide a really strong understanding of value in the overall supply chain – if the consumer stops buying, money will stop flowing at source!

On the other side of the equation is the total cost of ownership for the customer. This is not just the purchase price, but also the cost of maintaining the product and service and continuing to do work with you as a supplier. If this number is greater than the impact you provide, you are not providing value (and the customer will either buy from other suppliers or seek to beat you down on price).

Always sell and negotiate based on value creation. Failing to discuss value can lead to 'price-focused' bartering.

Figure 13.3 shows the main elements of a value proposition (this is a high-level statement that can be shared with the customer to bring the value equation to life). Value propositions should always lead with a simple statement of how the customer business state will improve in the future. Use the five sources of value to describe this.

- To back this up, there needs to follow descriptions of the offering. What will you provide to make this future state possible? Why should you be regarded as credible?

- The final support is a value appraisal. You should provide financial justification to describe payback, cost-effectiveness and key measures that can be used to track that you are delivering your 'value promises'.

- In essence, the customer value proposition is an exciting executive summary of a proposed business model that will occur between two parties that trade. In your supply chain, there will be multiple value propositions. The question for you is: 'What does each value proposition describe, and what does it do to my brand?

Figure 13.4 tries to map value potential. When an organization defends its position without a value discussion, it inevitably sinks to a price conversation. Value becomes finite (you can only drop your price so low; eventually you reach zero).

Figure 13.3   Three main components of a value proposition

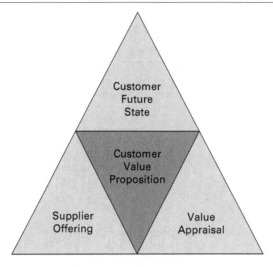

SOURCE Used with kind permission of Bloomsbury Business, an imprint of Bloomsbury Publishing plc

Figure 13.4   Finite or infinite value?

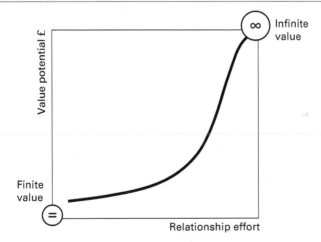

SOURCE Used with kind permission of Bloomsbury Business, an imprint of Bloomsbury Publishing plc

On the other hand, if you describe value in terms of what is really important to the customer, value can be infinite. In my BEMS story, I would have paid two to three times over the fee that we finally agreed if a supplier had assured me a fully validated system that would meet FDA standards. Think of it this way. If the £100,000 system failed and held up the overall project by two months, it delayed a £20 million project. It also stopped my site from making profits and possibly breaching supply contracts. This could be a multi-million-dollar figure (or even possible total withdrawal of

Figure 13.5   The channel tension

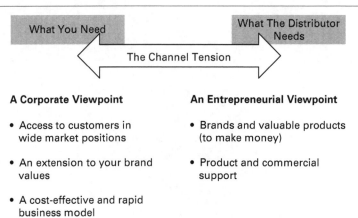

A Corporate Viewpoint	An Entrepreneurial Viewpoint
• Access to customers in wide market positions	• Brands and valuable products (to make money)
• An extension to your brand values	• Product and commercial support
• A cost-effective and rapid business model	

SOURCE Used with kind permission of Bloomsbury Business, an imprint of Bloomsbury Publishing plc

parent company confidence). And yet, nobody in the supply chain talked to me in these terms. The discussions were all about fees and contracts. Value discussions should have been about business reputation, continuity, risk and protecting my brand (and my job!).

Easing the value tensions in supply chains

In *Infinite Value*,[1] a book that I have written that describes principles of value-based selling and the supporting organization, I discuss a number of tensions that arise when businesses look to do business with customers on a longer-term 'value' basis. Tensions arise with this more complex business model: sales that may have been measured by quarter previously need to be tracked on a different time horizon – possibly over a period of years. The core offering also potentially shifts from products to products plus services (or even totally integrated solutions).

A tension also exists within the channels of the supply chain. As a larger organization, seeking an extension to your reach, the use of a supply chain is seen as a cost-effective option. Figure 13.5 shows the factors that cause a tension to possibly arise, with the supplier organization seeking efficiency and a cheaper supply chain, but the organizations that reside within the supply chain possibly being more entrepreneurial SMEs (small to medium enterprises). A good starting point when looking at a supply chain partner organization is to consider exactly who they are.

Figure 13.6   Third party channel relationships

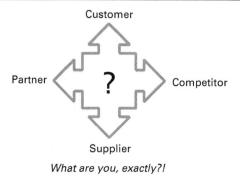

What are you, exactly?!

Figure 13.6 poses this question. Many organizations can look at the members of the supply chain and wonder what their role and relationship is. If they pay your bills, they could be regarded as a customer. If they supply part assemblies or resources, they could be a supplier; if they also provide a competitive product to the market, they could even be considered as a competitor. Partnerships are hollow gestures with supply chain organizations if you lack clarity and a common understanding of what you mean to each other. Ask yourself with each player:

> Exactly who are you to my organization, and how do you create (or destroy) the value I am taking to the market?

On a practical basis, it is also useful to stretch your understanding of what each member of the supply chain is doing. Think beyond the only option being 'a logistical extension to your reach'. Figure 13.6 shows how each member of the supply chain also provides commercial, technical, and potentially operational support. If this is the case, you really need to work very closely with them in order to develop a very clear understanding of the concepts of value, value-based selling, and specifically the value opportunities that are intrinsic within your brands and offering. If you fail to make this investment, channel partners will revert to the lowest common denominator of business – price – and this will destroy value.

Figure 13.7 is a useful schematic when considering the breadth of potential activities that supply chains can provide. Of course, they offer a distribution/logistics extension and network for organizations, offering local delivery of products. They also provide a cost-effective extension to commercial sales functions, and alongside this technical support. The fact

Figure 13.7   The role of channel partners

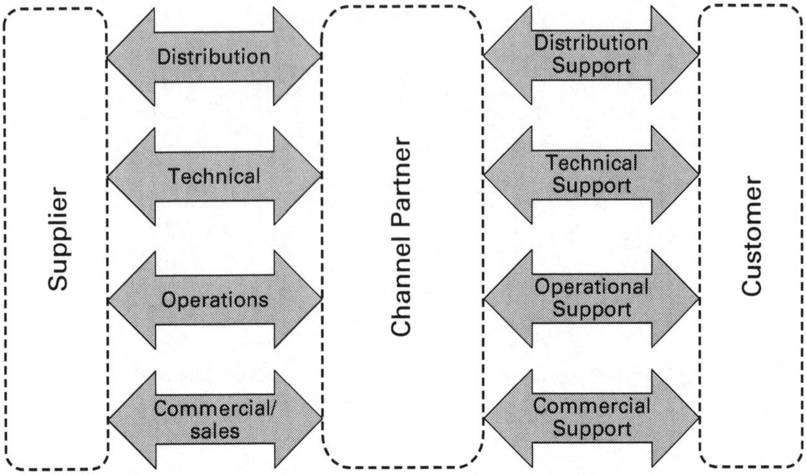

SOURCE   Used with kind permission of Bloomsbury Business, an imprint of Bloomsbury Publishing plc

that they value the customer base in the areas that they operate, and the local knowledge that they possess, often means that they can provide an enhanced service that the OEM supplier could.

Channel partners within the supply chain can also provide operational activities. I have seen supply chain organizations provide assembly, blending, repair centres, packaging services and local advising (in the case of professional services organizations).

This breadth, depth and quality of offering can position channel partners as customers, competitors and partners. It is not uncommon for organizations to look at the members of their supply chain and ask the question: *'Who are you, and what do you do?'*

Ten steps to build supply chain capability

To help with the development of a supply chain, the following 10-step process is provided. It splits into three parts – strategy, develop and operate – and while it is quite high level, it does provide a useful model to develop the supply chain, especially when you are looking to extend and maximize the reach of your value potential to the end-user customer.

Figure 13.8   Ten steps to build supply chain capability

1. Understand what you need
2. Segment and classify

Strategy   Develop

Operate

3. Start a dialogue
4. Agree partnerships
5. Select your team
6. Develop value models

7. Train, coach and develop
8. Build joint strategies
9. Share best practice – the channel partner alumni
10. Reflect

SOURCE Used with kind permission of Bloomsbury Business, an imprint of Bloomsbury Publishing plc

Step 1: understand what you need

Ask yourself the following questions to focus on your supply chain:

- What are the end-customers that we need to access?
- Where are they located?
- Do we have the existing commercial, technical, operational and logistical reach/capability to serve these customers?
- What do they need from the relationship with us?
- What do we need?
- What behaviour do we need from our channel partners? Do we get this today?
- What are the gaps in where we are today, versus where we need to get to?

Step 2: segment and classify

A segmentation model needs to be constructed. Classifying channel partners in terms of the impact they can have reaching your target customers, as well as the intent you both share working in partnership, are important foundation criteria to identify partners. Set out the channel partner segmentation model and allocate criteria to position partners into each segment.

This segmentation exercise will provide a first-cut picture indicating how the channel business could be constructed and the names of partners in each region/country.

Step 3: start a dialogue

The key word in all of this is 'partnership'. In particular, building a common strategy and understanding with the critical strategic channel partners requires a discussion. You select them because they seem to have the scale and fit to suit your needs. There has to be a mutual fit for them to work with you as well. This really is a conversation that has to take place – you need to seek agreement and a commitment to work together.

In situations where the channel partner does not see value in collaboration, you may have to reconsider appointing them as being strategic.

Step 4: agree partnerships

All partnerships should be agreed upon. This will be a combination of a service level agreement, and (possibly) more formal legal contracts. These should be drawn up and agreed between both parties. Getting this balance, between a vision of a new relationship and a formal contract, is obviously quite difficult. Try to fall on the side of partnership and be less formal.

Step 5: select your team (to manage the supply chain partners)

The managers and supporting teams that work with each channel partner should be carefully selected. A channel manager competency profile can be drawn up, and recruitment made against these profiles. Build your organization around each channel type – recognize that managing a strategic channel partner needs more dedicated focus than a channel associate. Establish guidelines such as one full-time equivalent (FTE) channel manager can look after no more than two strategic channel partners, while one FTE could look after 10 channel associate partners. Simple guidelines help to build the structure and set up names against each position.

It is also a good idea to develop main contacts and support teams with each channel partner organization. There needs to be a strong consistent relationship that develops over time. Naming teams on both sides of the relationship can really help.

Step 6: develop value models

Value models are the components that will be created and shared with the channel partner to enable them to transition to a value-centric business model. These should be considered and then developed as a series of capability standards that can be shared. When constructing these, it is a good idea to think, *'If I was running this channel business, what would I need to have in place to develop the required new ways of working?'*

Step 7: train, coach and develop

Implementing the new value-based principles means working with each channel partner and implementing ways of transferring the new business models. This could take the form of:

- an agreed series of training modules (direct and web-based);
- training via online modules;
- introduction of planning tools and agreeing ways to co-create customer value;
- facilitated workshops to help with strategy, segmentation and business plan development;
- leadership coaching.

These are all high-investment and time-consuming activities. It is critical to work with selected strategic channel associates that are committed to the new ways of working and will invest themselves in making the transition. Think about it: if you don't share your views and knowledge regarding value-based business with your supply chain partners, how else will they learn and develop?

Step 8: build joint strategies

Understanding the end-user customer and getting them to buy more products and services at more favourable fees and terms creates real value. This is only realized when you work with your channel partners to establish a stronger understanding of the customers that they reach (especially if they are serving your target key customers). Joint planning where you work with the channel partner team (consider commercial, technical, operational and supply chain aspects) will lead to stronger plans and improved business results for all parties.

Step 9: share best practice (the channel partner alumni)

Keeping value-based business alive with channel partners takes effort and constant re-energizing. While a series of training programmes and workshops will raise awareness and invigorate excitement, it will soon fall off the agenda if it is not fuelled and reminders provided to enable discussion and sharing of best practice stories.

Alumni organizations work really well for this. Set up a club or group, and once partners have been selected and go through initial stages of training and development – they can attend conferences and listen to online webinars, etc.

These can be very motivating and will be prized memberships for your channel partners (it can often be a motivational driver to get them to become a club member).

Step 10: reflect

Situations change in the market, and there is always the possibility that your initial thinking when setting up the channel strategy was not entirely correct. Constant reviewing of your strategy, the segmentation and selection of channel partners and results will highlight areas that you need to focus on in the future. Be prepared to repeat the cycle of strategy, develop and operate.

Ten tips to help you create value with your supply chain

The following can be offered as advice when you are looking at supplying your products and services. These are based on the reflection from this BEMS case study, and from other examples that I have been directly involved with as an advisor and consultant.

1 Have a 'value cell' philosophy

It is easy to sit back and look at the end-user as your customer and that your products and brands will be sufficient on their own to drive growth. That may be the case in the early stages of new products, but when they are copied and matched by competitor offerings, that value potential will diminish. The supply chain can be a source of competitive advantage, but it needs to be developed strategically and carefully. Have a value-cell philosophy, alongside your value-selling capability.

2 Map your supply chain

Figure 13.1 showed a simple supply chain model for my BEMS story. In reality, the supply chain can be more complex. That should not stop you from modelling all of the key players in the supply chain. Include the suppliers to your business as well as competitors. While the supply chain map may end up looking complex and messy, at least you will have a picture of the battlefield you are operating within.

Table 13.1 shows an analysis of the BEMS supply chain story – modelled as an example. The table is constructed by listing four columns across the top that represent the three elements of a value proposition plus a comment on what is happening overall. The vertical rows list out the various organizations that make up the supply chain.

It is a fairly simple technique, but makes you model what is happening at each stage, and draws out the main commercial aspects between each relationship. From the analysis in Table 13.1 it can be seen that while the panel builders, M&E contractor and design and build contractor all provide quality and technical expertise, the nature of how they are commercially connected to the supply chain is to meet contractual/fee-reducing activities. This can erode the initial value proposition that is intended by the OEM supplier to the end-user. Unless there is intervention to discuss and focus on total value in use, the supply chain can destroy value (and the OEM supplier will realize a lower overall fee).

These supply chain analysis tables can capture a lot of information, but splitting the value proposition information out, as per this example, starts to help gain an understanding of why commercial decisions are made.

3 Put yourself in their shoes

When supply chains 'fragment' and two to three organizations start working with each other in isolation, it can be frustrating to observe these dynamics and criticize the way that the supply chain is destroying your value. To understand this better, take some time out. Go and speak to managers in each organization and try to understand why they are making the commercial decisions that they do. You may be surprised, but at least you will start to understand how they think and why they behave the way that they do.

Table 13.1 Supply chain value proposition analysis

	Value (future state)	Offer description	Value appraisal	Activity description
OEM (BEMS) supplier	Offer reliable products and services save energy (Can be validated to FDA Standards)	Strong brand. High R&D spend. The best hardware and software available.	Specification. Performance. Brand	Designer and manufacturer of world-class BEMS systems. Market-leading technology
Panel builders	Technicians develop systems to meet the contractual specifications	Build and install control panels on time and within budget	Quality. Cost	Challenge: Working under a strict cost-based contract from M&E contractor
M&E contractor	The design, build and installation of complex building utility systems - as per contractual terms	Designers and contract experts will develop the DETAIL utility systems for the facility. Driven by cost savings	Project management. Cost. Time	Challenge: Working under a strict cost-based contract from Design & Build contractor
Design & build contractor	Design and build a facility on time and under cost	Focus on specifying a complex building. Building and delivering to strict schedule	Project management. Cost. Time	Challenge: Working under a strict cost-based contract from M&E contractor
Customer (end user)	An FDA standard and approved pharmaceutical manufacturing facility is required	This is the first facility of this type in the world. It must be built to pharmaceutical standards	Performance. Quality. Standards and Reliability	Needs facility to be VALIDATED and available for use at set date

4 Describe the value proposition between each party

When you are having these conversations, either ask directly or (if it is difficult) make assumptions about what the organization's value proposition is to their direct customer. Do they talk about value correctly, or do they simply talk about a 'cheaper alternative'? Taking the time to model the value proposition at each stage can really introduce understanding about the overall dynamics in your supply chain. Table 13.1 can help with this.

5 Ask the supply chain what they think of you

You don't want to appear to be taking a high position in the conversations you are having with supply chain partners. Taking a more collegiate stance will lead to more open discussions and open feedback. Ask the people that you speak to for their feedback on your organization. Are you a good supplier? Do they get effective technical/commercial and market advice? What could you do to make their life better (and help them to make more money!)?

6 Preach value

Many larger organizations take the time to understand the concept of value and to assess how they conduct value-based selling, account management and pricing. Many organizations within the supply chain are smaller, more entrepreneurial organizations. They may never have considered what value is or what it means to them. Talking value and providing training sessions is often really appreciated. Be obsessed. Talk about value and spend the time working with your supply chain to understand and start working in this different way.

7 Hold value seminars

To really put your money where your mouth is, it is a great idea to hold regular conferences, seminars and workshops. Make this a two-way discussion by encouraging supply chain members to present and showcase examples where they have created and delivered value propositions into the market. These conferences should be managed carefully (there is always the need for competition laws to be observed) – but as long as you design this in, they will reap significant benefits and generate very thought-provoking discussions.

8 Change the conversation

When you want to discuss big value opportunities, you have to change the conversation. This means talking to increasingly senior people. When I was acting as the end-user customer in my BEMS story, I was a senior director and on the leadership team. I was open to discussing my challenges and what I needed and valued. Imagine the benefits you would have if you could have those conversations with 10–20 senior executives right across your supply chain. It would lead to incredibly powerful information, but you would have to have brave, open and reciprocating conversations with some challenging, senior people.

9 Look backwards

The concept of being 'customer-centric' is often portrayed as an essential for proactive business. It is true: you do need to focus on the customer. But you should also see your suppliers as partners and sources of value collaboration. Be 'value-centric' and look to help everybody in your supply chain, especially your suppliers (how hypocritical would it be not to behave like that, anyway?).

10 Value co-create (collaborate and thrive)

Many organizations are looking to collaborate as they seek increasingly new products and services to compete in aggressive global markets. Organizations often seek new partners or even competitors to work with. All the time, however, you could have a willing and highly capable set of partners that you already work with: your supply chain. You just need to view the supply chain as a source of significant competitive advantage by focusing on 'end-to-end' value creation.

Reference

1   Davies, M (2017) *Infinite Value: Accelerating profitable growth through value-based selling*. Bloomsbury Publishing, London.

Financial analysis, value quantification tools and financial dashboards

14

This book is not about financial analysis but it is important that we consider ROI, IRR, NPV, and payback in order to give credibility to the purchasing company and comfort to their finance director. There are plenty of models available, some of which are free, and it is important that you engage with your own finance department in order to make sure that the models that you're developing stand up to scrutiny.

In the six-step value proposition process that was mentioned earlier in the book, in step four we talked about categorizing the value that can be achieved for the supplier. In the box below, we show that the three factors that should be considered are: added value, which is normally revenue gains, cost avoidance and cost reduction. Much of the focus is on cost reduction because this is often the easiest of the three factors to identify and manage.

Do you have value proposition models that the potential customer believes?

Financial calculations should be based on three factors:

1 added value (functional, eg revenue gains);

2 cost avoidance;

3 cost reduction.

> A fourth relates to the intangible benefits, such as reputation, trust, and risk reduction (harder to quantify). In this respect, powerful branding is important. Market segmentation, however, is the key to this crucial element of differentiation.

The second box is an example we have worked on and it was the introduction of job scheduling software for a maintenance team. We identified the cost savings, which were £250,000 per annum. We identified the cost avoidance by not having to buy a new fleet of vehicles, with an £80,000 saving, and finally we were able to identify that by reducing these costs they were far more competitive in the external market and were able to win two new contracts valued at £1 million of revenue.

Value proposition job scheduling software maintenance team

1 **Cost reduction** – staff numbers reduced from 30 to 22 and the number of jobs increased by 30 per cent with 8 fewer staff. In addition, cut down on travel costs. Savings £250,000 per annum.

2 **Cost avoidance** – rearranged the van fleet and sold the old vans that were becoming costly in terms of maintenance. Avoid buying more vans as fewer people were needed. £80,000 per year saving.

3 **Revenue increase** – bid for additional external contracts with more confidence, as the cost base was under control and were very competitive. Won two new contracts valued £1,000,000.

Let us now go back and look at the issue of ROI, IRR, NPV and payback. Using spreadsheets, these numbers are easy to calculate, but it is important that the suppliers understand what is meant and confirm the factors that are driving the customer's business. Some customers are interested just in payback. Does the investment produce a payback in less than 12 months? Other customers are looking at ROI (return on investment) and will expect it to be at least 100 per cent. For ROI to be 100 per cent means that for every pound invested in the project, it will generate £2.

The definitions below have been adapted from an article with kind permission from Tom Pisello at TechTarget – The ROI Guy, CEO and Founder at Aliean Inc. See: Blog.alinean.com[1]

Each of these figures – payback, discounted payback, NPV, ROI and IRR – try to summarize a set of cash flows from a project into a single indicator. But like the dashboard on your car, one figure alone cannot tell you the entire investment story. Each has their intended purpose and strengths and weaknesses.

Payback

Payback is one of the most common ways to assess the value of a project. Payback is calculated by comparing the cumulative cash investment in the project and comparing it against the cumulative benefits, typically month by month in a timeline. Most projects have a significant up-front investment, and then over time, this investment is recouped post-deployment with benefits. Eventually, the benefits catch up to and exceed the initial and ongoing investments required. The duration from initial investment to the point where the cumulative benefits exceed the costs is the payback period. Most teams like to see paybacks within 12 months or less, and some are even more demanding. Thus, one of the issues with using this as the sole determination of the project's worthiness is that it can get the team focused on projects that only offer quick paybacks, without regard to longer-term or more strategic investments. On the positive side, payback is often a good gauge for risk, whereby projects with longer payback periods are typically more risky – sensitive to cost overruns and delays at realizing planned values within the analysis horizon.

Discounted payback

Discounted payback takes the time value of money into account. When an investment is made in a project today, that investment needs to return more in the future because £1 today is worth more than £1 in the future, since we live in an inflationary world. One must also consider that this £1 could have been invested elsewhere, especially in less risky investment vehicles, so not only does a £1 investment have to compete with inflation, but it competes with other opportunities. Thus, to really break even, £1 today has to return more a year from now, and even more two, three and four years down the road (as interest compounds).

With a discounted payback period, the costs and benefits of the project are discounted as they occur over time to take into account the lost opportunity of investing the cash elsewhere (usually set equal to a company's cost of capital) and further by a relative measure of the project's risk (the cost of capital + a risk generated discount rate). For projects with long payback periods, discounted payback periods are more accurate at determining the real payback, but for shorter projects, a non-discounted payback period is normally a good enough indicator. As with regular payback periods, making investment decisions based purely on these can orient the team towards quick payback projects without regard to the ultimate benefit quantity – which is best measured using NPV.

ROI and risk-adjusted ROI

This calculates the net benefits (total benefits – total costs) of a project divided by the total costs in a ratio to help highlight the magnitude of potential returns versus costs. An ROI of 150 per cent means that £1 invested in the project will garner the investor £1 of their original investment back plus £1.50 in gains. Risk-adjusted ROI is the recommended ratio to use, and it tallies using the time value of money to discount the benefits and costs over time. Risk-adjusted ROI provides a more conservative ratio, since benefits are usually higher than costs in outgoing years, thus the benefits are discounted and the ratio lower. Companies typically expect ROI of at least 100 per cent to usually not more than 400 per cent (although higher is possible). The ROI formula is great at comparing the costs to benefits in a ratio, but does not highlight well the timeliness of the returns, where payback period is more appropriate.

NPV

NPV is a formula that tallies all of the net benefits of a project (benefits – costs), adjusting all results into today's money terms. This is different from just tallying up all of the net benefits of a project over a three-year period without discounting, as the cumulative benefits without discounting overstate the overall project value, especially when the project has many of the investment costs up front or in year one and the benefits are not really kicking in until later years (where the time-value of money discounting reduces the overall value of these benefits). Net present value (NPV) is great at tallying up the net benefits over an investment horizon so that different projects can be compared with the value they return to the company, but this metric alone does not highlight how long it may take to achieve the benefits (as payback period does). Nor does it highlight the ratio of the costs versus the net benefits, which is where the ROI formula shines.

IRR

IRR is one of the best metrics for comparing projects. Internal rate of return (IRR) is essentially the interest rate that the project can generate for the company, and is calculated as the discount value that when applied in the NPV formula drives the NPV formula to zero. Since IRR calculates the cash flow return for each project, investments in projects can be compared easily with other investment vehicles and with investment hurdle rates (returns versus risks) established by the CFO. But IRR is not a great indicator as to the magnitude of investment needed, benefit value or payback, so the returns may be high, but the investment high, benefits not significant and/or payback (risk) too high.

Value chain model

As you can see, no one metric highlights all of the value strengths, weaknesses and risks of a given investment, especially when comparing several options. We recommend that you use several of these indicators in conjunction – including risk-adjusted ROI, payback period, NPV and IRR – along with investment required, risk score and business alignment score when assessing projects.

Let's go back to the value chain model that we have previously discussed and the financial numbers that can be developed (see Table 14.1). These can then be categorized into revenue gains, cost avoidance and cost reduction.

Figures 14.1 and 14.2 show two examples of financial models and different ways of presenting the results.

In Figure 14.1, the numbers are presented in a simple dashboard. In Figure 14.2, we can see that SKF have built very sophisticated models that will produce detailed proposals for the customer automatically. Your sales team will need to be trained on exactly what the results mean so they can have sensible discussions with the customer.

Table 14.1 Financially quantified value propositions workshop summary

Customer's value chain weaknesses and opportunities for the supplier to add value		Customer weaknesses	Describe in words the opportunity for us (the supplier)	Importance to the customer or impact (high/med/low)	Added value ($ € £)	Cost reduction ($ € £)	Cost avoidance ($ € £)	Intangible benefits ($ € £)
VALUE CHAIN	Inbound							
	Operations							
	Outbound							
	Marketing and sales							
	Customer service							
VALUE CHAIN FIRM INFRASTRUCTURE	Finance							
	Procurement							
	Technology development							
	HR management							
	Other (e.g. CSR)							

Subtotal:

TOTAL: $ € £

Figure 14.1 Financial models

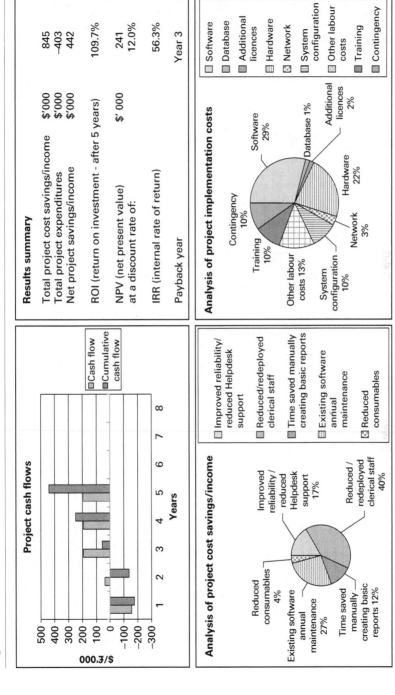

Results summary

Total project cost savings/income	$'000	845
Total project expenditures	$'000	-403
Net project savings/income	$'000	442
ROI (return on investment - after 5 years)		109.7%
NPV (net present value) at a discount rate of:	$' 000	241
		12.0%
IRR (internal rate of return)		56.3%
Payback year		Year 3

Project cash flows

- Cash flow
- Cumulative cash flow

Analysis of project implementation costs

Software 29%
Database 1%
Additional licences 2%
Hardware 22%
Network 3%
System configuration 10%
Other labour costs 13%
Training 10%
Contingency 10%

- Software
- Database
- Additional licences
- Hardware
- Network
- System configuration
- Other labour costs
- Training
- Contingency

Analysis of project cost savings/income

Reduced / redeployed clerical staff 40%
Improved reliability / reduced Helpdesk support 17%
Time saved manually creating basic reports 12%
Existing software annual maintenance 27%
Reduced consumables 4%

- Improved reliability/ reduced Helpdesk support
- Reduced/redeployed clerical staff
- Time saved manually creating basic reports
- Existing software annual maintenance
- Reduced consumables

Figure 14.2   Example for SKF

Spend minutes. Save thousands.   **SKF**

SKF Documented Solutions

SKF Y-units food line (Marathon)

The food and beverage market offers enormous growth potential, being one of the largest manufacturing and distribution sector segments in the economy. The processed food market itself grows almost at 10% per year, and has been growing at this rate for the past 25 years. The reasons of such a growth? An increased per capita income, lifestyle changes and technological innovations made necessary by world food safety trends. SKF has decided to apply its know-how, quality standards and research results on materials and technologies to create a wide range of high quality solutions in this demanding market. The result is a line of products that combines high resistance, advanvced technology and extended service life.

Documented value	
Description	**Value**
Value added over MTBR (8.00 Months)	37657.45 $
Expected ROI over MTBR	390.23 %
Cash flow break-even	2.43 Months
Break-even MTBR increase percentage necessary	142.79 %
Break-even MTBR increase in months necessary	1.43 Months

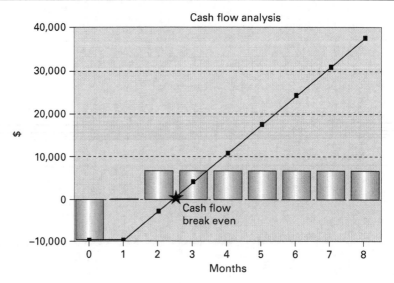

Defining the numbers for improving sales and marketing and scenario-building

We have discussed the sales formula previously and the impact that small improvements in adopting a quantified value proposition process can have on revenues.

There are five factors that impact how much you sell. It is a function of:

1 number of leads;

2 closure rate;

3 frequency of purchase;

4 average deal size;

5 sales cycle.

Marketing has most influence on item 1 and the sales team have most influence on items 2 to 5 (see Figure 14.3).

Only 5 per cent of companies have financially quantified value propositions (McKinsey) and developing them will differentiate your company. Even if you don't have any differentiation, the very act of financially quantifying the benefits, even if they are standard benefits, will give you an advantage over your competitors. It will help make marketing campaigns more productive and increase the number of leads generated. More deals will be closed (typically an additional 2–10 per cent) and it will help reduce discounting (by 20–30 per cent) and thus improve deal size. In addition, the sales cycle will be reduced by 10–25 per cent.[2]

There are additional benefits that are harder to quantify:

- avoidance of no/delayed decisions to buy;
- improved customer relationships;
- referrals from satisfied customers;
- sustained relationships.

Figure 14.3   Sales formula and sales process

$$\text{Sales Formula} = \frac{(1) \text{ Number of leads} \times (2) \text{ Closure rate (\%)} \times (3) \text{ Frequency of Purchase} \times (4) \text{ Average Deal Size (£)}}{(5) \text{ Sales Cycle (months)}}$$

SOURCE Based on the Sales Velocity Equation, reproduced with the kind permission of Donal Daly, Executive Chairman at Altify (formerly The TAS Group)

If we take the sales formula in Figure 14.3 and apply some standard numbers for the software industry, we can see the impact in Table 14.2 and Figure 14.4.

This model will typically generate sales of £1,000,000 per month.

We can then consider a 5 per cent improvement for all the factors in Table 14.3 and we see the revenue increase by 28 per cent per month, as shown in Figure 14.5.

Table 14.2   Sales formula

Sales formula – five factors	Current situation
1 Number of leads per month	125
2 Closure rate	20%
3 Frequency of purchase	1
4 Average deal size	£120,000
5 Sales cycle in months	3 months

Figure 14.4   Sales formula current situation

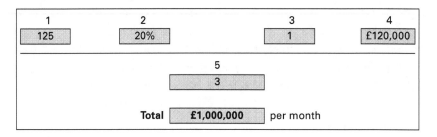

Table 14.3   Sales formula with 5 per cent improvement

Sales formula – five factors	Current situation	5% improvement in all factors
1 Number of leads per month	125	131.25
2 Closure rate	20%	21%
3 Frequency of purchase	1	1.05
4 Average deal size	£120,000	£126,000
5 Sales cycle in months	3 months	2.85 months

Figure 14.5   Sales formulae with 5 per cent improvement

By working through the numbers with the sales and marketing team, we have then come up with the specific improvements for the five factors, as shown in Table 14.4. The company knows that it is poor compared with the industry in some areas and the targets are shown below.

By calculating the specific improvements for all the five factors as shown in Table 14.4, we see the revenue increase is 35 per cent per month, as shown in Figure 14.6.

In summary, this model can be used at the beginning of your quantified value proposition project for your company in order to target improvements. Here we hand over to Alan Crean at Changepoint, a subject matter expert in the quote-to-cash lifecycle for services and consultancy firms, with huge thanks for a brilliant contribution on this topic.

Table 14.4   Sales formula with specific improvements

Sales formula – five factors	Current Situation	5% improvement in all factors	Specific improvements
1 Number of leads per month	125	131.25	137.5 (10%)
2 Closure rate	20%	21%	21% (5%)
3 Frequency of purchase	1	1.05	1 (0%)
4 Average deal size	£120,000	£126,000	£126,000 (5%)
5 Sales cycle in months	3 months	2.85 months	2.7 months (10%)

Figure 14.6   Sales formula with specific improvements

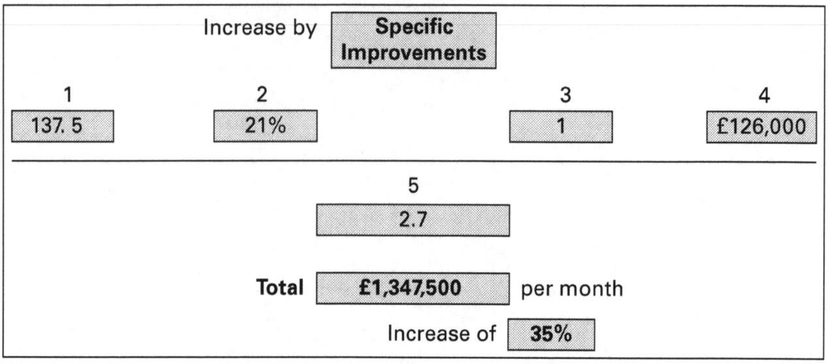

An ROI contribution from the industry

Contributed by Alan Crean, Business Unit Executive at Changepoint PSC and PPM in EMEA, a professional services automation (PSA) application designed for cost-based projects

It is your ROI too

ROI has two sides to it. There is the ROI for the customer of buying the deal; there is also the ROI of your organization taking on the deal.

The ROI of the sales effort

Your time as an account manager requires an ROI. As such, a quick look at the information below will give you a view as to where time is best spent. This data is particular to the professional services industry, but the numbers for every industry are similar. From the results shown in Figure 14.7, we should encourage existing customers to make introductions to other potential customers and identify the customers that need problems solved.

Present an ROI in terms of what they do not have, not what they get – use scenarios based on averages and/ or percentages

Below is an actual business case that was presented to a potential customer. It was delivered to a group who already knew that they wanted a solution,

Figure 14.7   Cold calls, leads and referrals

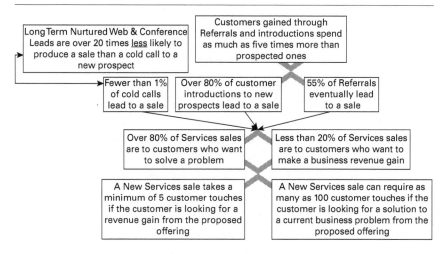

so there was no point in shooting ourselves in the foot by coming up with an unbelievable business case on ROI, especially as they would have tied us to it. In order to understand how the financial model is built up, let's discuss the key factors in Table 14.5 based on the company's sales of $142,680,000 per annum and 580 billable staff.

Support and management staff costs generally equate to approximately 22 per cent, billable staff costs average 58 per cent, while process costs equate to 12 per cent, property to 5 per cent, and general assets to 3 per cent. Note that we said *generally*. It's easy to include a word that shows you know enough to make a point, without knowing all the numbers in finite detail. The rule here is simple: never, ever argue with an accountant.

Table 14.5   Estimated revenue gains and cost reduction

Summary table	Revenue gains	Cost reduction
Billable staff	$1,230,000	$650,000
Administration pool		$45,000
Management		$180,000
Customer billing		$81,905
Paper and consumable costs		$10,000
Backlog increased	$998,760	
Written off days	$2,271,000	
Realization rate	$1,426,800	

However, if you convert the fact that the billable staff are the ones who earn the revenue, and that the average is 164 (63 per cent of 261) billable days per year, a 1 per cent increase equates to 820 extra billable days in a year.

Revenue gain: 820 days @ $1,500 a day = $1,230,000

The rule here is that you can use the word *average*, but only if you have read, experienced, and understood enough to take in general numbers about your industry. Be prepared for them to ask where you came up with the average number, but the nice thing is that it's defensible either from an industry or from other customer benchmarks.

But the financial accounting way of looking at this is that you now need 1 per cent less staff to deliver this work. 820 days at 164 working days per annum is five fewer people. A cost per employee at the daily realization rate of $1,500 would be about $130,000 a year.

Cost saving: 5 x $130,000 = $650,000

We have used the same data set twice here. This is as a protection mechanism. So we said that you could either go up by $1,230,000 in revenue, or down $650,000 in cost. Both are true, but you can only have one or the other, and human nature is that both are mentally counted.

Now let's look at the administration pool, which is almost 100 across the entire business. The average salary cost is $45,000 and they work a 40-hour week each. Therefore, giving a cost per hour over the 45 working weeks a year, they do work of $25 an hour. If we can make them 1 per cent more efficient across the 1,800 hours each that they work, that would be the equivalent of giving the company back one full salary of $45,000.

Cost saving: $45,000

Never, ever go more than 1 per cent when you talk about efficiency gains in people. For a start, it's never evenly spread across a group, and second, it is not a true cost benefit or saving in the eyes of a CEO of CFO.

There are 120 staff at management grade. These would have an average cost of $150,000 across the business. Using the same metrics as the administration staff, that would be $180,000 saved.

Cost saving: $180,000

Again, the 1 per cent rule. It is defensible, it's always seen as a minimum, it's easily understood, and it focuses on the benefit without having to commit to a number. Now let's consider the customer billing. The firm has an annual revenue of $142,680,000 and an average 'day sales outstanding' of 67 days. So at any one time, it would have $5,487,692 of outstanding invoices. As we cannot parse a day, we are looking at a reduction of just one day in this area.

So if the firm could move to an average of 66 days, that would equate to an additional $81,905 in the bank.

Cost saving: $81,905

Doing a 'you get paid quicker' is great, but it fails the ROI test. The reason is simple: money in the bank has no more value than money owed when it comes to the balance sheet. So all I have done is move money from one column to another, nothing fundamentally changed, and a CFO will know that.

If you also consider that a 1 per cent reduction in the volume of paper, mains water, and cleaning chemicals used was to happen, that would also impact the bottom line – and industry pundits proclaim that would have a $10,000 effect on a business this size.

Cost saving: $10,000

It is always good to include a number from someone else, but never a big one – the only person a CIO trusts less than a sales person is the analyst who tells him how everyone else is better, faster and more efficient than he is.

This firm is billing $35,670,000 a quarter in revenues. As an average firm, it is entering each new quarter with 70 per cent of that already in backlog. If backlog increased by 1 per cent, that would yield an additional $998,760 per annum in sales.

Revenue gain: $998,760

Again, the 1 per cent number to keep us from anything that looks like we have to make an obligation on achieved value. It's not that we do not want the client to get the value; it's that we do not want to commit to one as that would cause us some revenue recognition issues. And nothing will stop you getting your commission cheque faster than a revenue recognition query.

As an average firm, they are also writing off days per annum from late delivered projects and work performed without commercial cover. That industry number average is debated at being 4 per cent, which would equate to 10.44 days per billable consultant. If we use a 1 per cent reduction, which is 2.61 days per billable consultant (580), we can generate 1,514 days at $1,500 per day, equal to $2,271,000 in unbilled days a year.

Figure 14.8   Financial models – dashboard

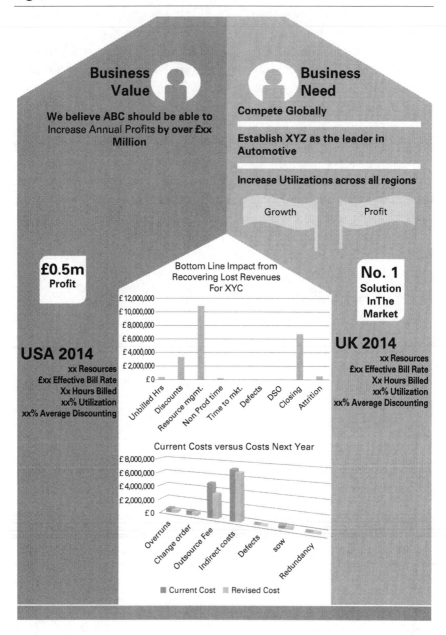

Revenue gain: $2,271,000

We use average and we use 1 per cent. We did not use these to avoid an issue, more to emphasize that the problem of achieving that saving is the client's and not mine. We can give them a great tool or system, but we cannot make them a good manager of their business.

And then there is the realization rate – the net amount actually billed for each consultant. If you could drive that up by 1 per cent (a mere $15 a day), you would increase company revenues by $1,426,800 a year.

Revenue gain: $1,426,800

Again, 1 per cent to make it a discussion rather than a fact.

In summary, it is then a question on deciding which of the numbers in the table are the most credible and categorizing them into either revenue gains or cost savings, but not both. The supplier will then identify the solution required and the appropriate costs and build the financial model. This supplier then produces very sophisticated models and presents the outputs in Figure 14.8 based on the input from the potential customer.

Actions

Complete Table 14.1 and complete the sales formula for your organization in Table 14.2 and Table 14.3. Work with your own finance team to produce a credible ROI model.

References

1 http://blog.alinean.com/2010/08/return-on-investment-roi-defined.html

2 For references to justify the percentages quoted, see Michael Nick (2018) *Why do you need ROI in your sales process?* 22 February. Available at: http://www.roi4sales.com/roi/what-is-the-roi-on-roi-anyway/ [Last accessed 22 June 2018].

Summary of the value proposition process 15

In earlier chapters we have discussed the various steps of the value proposition process, which are shown below in Figure 15.1, and we will refer to the appropriate chapters for each of the six steps.

Figure 15.1 Value proposition process

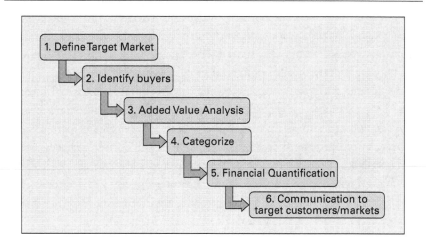

Step 1: define the target market

In Chapter 2 we start on the journey of defining the target market and we discuss at some length market segmentation, which is the bedrock of profitable growth. We discussed the product market table, which will then allow you to think about the level at which you describe value propositions. There is an extremely useful exercise for generating market segments and this has been tried and tested on a very large number of business-to-business (B2B) companies.

Chapter 4 gives an overview of the process and where to start and ties in this value proposition process with strategic marketing planning and key account management planning. It has further sections on defining the target market and again refers to this very useful product market table. In addition, we take you through the steps of the market map, which again has been used extensively and helps companies define the way in which the market works, from suppliers through distributors to retailers and finally to end-users.

Step 2: identify buyers

Chapter 5, entitled 'Why it is critical to understand how key buying decisions are made', is in two parts. The first deals with how major customers buy and the second part deals with how other customers purchase. This gives you great insight into the way that key accounts make buying decisions and, in addition, the process typically used by the mass market to buy. It is important to understand that value propositions need to be targeted at market segments which consist of groups of customers of the same or similar needs. We also develop the thinking around who the decision-makers are and how frequently these people need to be communicated to.

In Chapter 6 we discussed for which key accounts you should develop value propositions. It is important to decide which of these are strategic. We should spend our time and effort on these strategic accounts where we know that there are opportunities to sell additional products and services, rather than on the key accounts which are driven purely by price.

Having identified the key accounts, Chapter 7 helps the reader to also identify mid-sized B2B customers by their potential to succeed based on a questionnaire developed at Cranfield School of Management.

Step 3: added value analysis

Chapter 8 helps us to understand the needs of the selected accounts and helps us to develop further the identification of some of the added value analysis that can be addressed in the customer base. In Figure 8.8 we provide further details on the concept of the value chain; this is fundamental to developing quantified value propositions. We develop further the value chain process and how this can be broken down into quantified sections. The tools in Chapter 10 will allow you to quantify the value chain analysis.

Chapter 10 helps us to think through the development of value propositions for market segments and we are also introduced to a very useful case study. In chapter 10 we are taken through the process to put figures against what we see as the opportunities in Table 10.3.

Step 4: categorize

Chapter 3 discusses what exactly a financially quantified value proposition is and explains in detail the three components of a value proposition. In addition, examples from a software provider, SKF and a label company, are highlighted to identify the benefits.

Having completed the tables in Chapter 10, we are then in a position to categorize these savings into the following three headings:

1 revenue increases;

2 cost avoidance;

3 cost savings.

We categorize into the three headings above because it is then easier for the customer to understand the groupings that we have taken and it is also then a simple process to represent the figures in the financial model.

Step 5: financial quantification

The financial results come from quantifying the three categories of revenue increase, cost avoidance and cost saving. We are then able to start building the model based on any additional purchase expense that the customer may need to incur. In these models we are able to easily demonstrate the payback period, return on investment, net present value and finally the internal rate of return.

The financial results, as we saw in Chapter 14, can easily be set up in a spreadsheet. It is important, however, to ensure that your own finance department works with you on these models to ensure that the numbers are sound and that there is a credible answer.

It is also possible for new projects to establish the time to completion, as it may take several months to implement the working methods of the new system. It is also worth calculating the potential cost of waiting, ie what's the monthly cost that your customer experiences as a result of not purchasing your product or service? In our experience it certainly concentrates the thoughts of the customer and will help speed up the decision-making process.

Step 6: communication to target customers/markets

We mentioned websites in Chapter 1 and the need to revisit them and redevelop them. It is important that websites are owned by the marketing department and not put together by the website developer. They don't understand marketing, and the marketing department needs to have significant input into the design.

Over the years we have seen a number of financial models and we have developed a number of return on investment calculators on websites. The lessons we have learned are that these can be extremely dangerous because, first, it may give too much information away to your competitor, and second, they are often used inappropriately by customers. They can give misleading results and do not necessarily produce a credible response without input from the supplier. The recommendation is that you should certainly communicate that quantified value propositions are available for target customers and target markets. It is often better to put together a white paper or case study rather than allowing the customer to do the calculation themselves. We have mentioned SKF on a number of occasions; if you go to their website,[1] they explain the documented programme solution in great detail and give excellent examples. SKF request that potential customers talk to them so that an experienced account manager can construct an appropriate and credible model for them.

Summary

In summary we have touched on all six steps of the value proposition process. Some steps have been addressed in much more detail than others, as some of the steps are quite straightforward and simple. More experienced suppliers will have models available where they will go through a set of well-thought-through and standard questions in order to establish and validate information from the customer. This will then generate a credible model.

The very sophisticated suppliers will then have models that will automatically generate a proposal and will even download the pertinent points, particularly graphs and the summary, into PowerPoint presentations. These models can take some time to produce but we know from the market leader in this area that the potential benefits for doing this work are enormous. In Chapter 12, Todd Snelgrove discusses what SKF have developed; it has over 77,000 cases of approved customer value, which is equivalent to US$7 billion in value.

Many thanks for reading and we wish you much success!

Reference

1 http://www.skf.com/uk/knowledge-centre/engineering-tools/
skfdocumentsolutionsprogram.html

INDEX